when dreams come true

DISCOVER
A LOVE
WORTH
WAITING FOR

eric and leslie ludy

LOYAL PUBLISHING
www.loyalpublishing.com

WHEN DREAMS COME TRUE
Copyright © 2000 by Eric and Leslie Ludy
ISBN 1929125-17-8
Loyal Publishing, Inc.
P.O. Box 1892, Sisters, OR 97759

Front photo by Kim Butts.
Back photo by Andy Katz.
Cover design by Kent D. Estell.

01 02 03 04 05 / 10 9 8 7 6 5 4 3 2

To Our Parents:

Richard and Janet Runkles
Win and Barb Ludy

You have made us who we are today,
and we owe you our deepest gratitude.

Table of Contents

Part Three: the love story

Acknowledgments

Writing a book is like building a house from scratch; it always takes twice as long as you expect, and it is an all-consuming project until it is done! To the people in our life who have lovingly put up with us when we go into our "writing tunnel" and to those who have gone above and beyond the call of duty to make the whole process easier and more enjoyable, we owe a special thanks:

To WIN AND BARB LUDY: your tireless work at "Winston House" has given us the freedom to be creative. Your caring and giving spirit always lifts us out of the "sludge." Thank you for your patience, hard work and enthusiasm!

To RICH AND JANET RUNKLES: your listening ears and expert advice have carried us through both the ups and downs of this ministry. Thank you for the faithful prayer and practical help that you so readily and willingly offer whenever we need it.

To MARY JO GENTERT: Without you, this book would never have gotten finished! You may never realize just how much your life and servant's heart has meant to us. Thank you for so freely giving of your time, talent and love to bless us.

To THE TEAM AT LOYAL PUBLISHING: we so appreciate all the hard work you do behind the scenes to help make the whole process of releasing a book flow smoothly. We are so thankful God has allowed us to join up with teammates like you. It's exciting to work together to help spread a message of hope and truth to this world.

Authors' Note

Our families always groan when we release a new book. "I don't remember it happening that way!" is a typical response from at least one of our parents or siblings whenever they scrutinize a new manuscript. "That Toyota Camry was maroon, not red!" is an argument common around our family table as they scan through our story with wary eye.

Even Leslie and I disagree on some of the tiny details when we relive the moments of our lives and peer into our past. "Are you sure that conversation happened in the Ludy living room? I thought it was driving down I-25 in the Camry!" We spout back and forth and, more often than not, are forced to look back to old journal entries in order to come up with the most accurate account possible. But in spite of the careful eyes of our family members and the wonderful asset of our old journals, there are always those few details that remain "foggy" to our memory.

What you are about to read is a true story. It is a real-life account of the amazing things God did in our lives not too many years ago. We have changed many names and places to protect certain individuals' privacy. And though the events are actual, many details have been added to maintain the quality of the story. For example, we may not remember whether or not we really had hamburgers and potato salad the night our two families met in the Ludy kitchen. And we may not be one-hundred percent certain if it was a mustard stain, or if it was really pizza sauce that was the culprit behind Marky's blue shirt disaster. Admittedly, it is debatable whether or not I really rescued a doomed ladybug at that oh-so-crucial moment on the grassy hill. (I would like to believe I did!)

Though questions like this may remain unanswered, the truth of God's amazing faithfulness in our lives is the same today as it was then. This book was not designed to be a detailed account of our lives, but rather a beautiful look inside the very heart of God.

As you read this book, you may be sure that, beyond the peripheral details, the story is taken from actual fact. There might be moments while reading this story you may be tempted to think circumstances in our lives were "too good to be true" such as having godly parents who were able to provide us with wise counsel. But we do not in any way want to imply that discovering a God-written love story is conditional upon things like growing up in a Christian home. Through this book, we hope to convey that anyone can discover something beautiful in this area . . . by simply turning their lives over to the original Author of true love.

We invite you now to sit back and be encouraged, inspired, challenged and blessed as you laugh with us, cry with us, and walk with us as we relive our incredible journey to discover a love that was truly worth waiting for.

The Day a Dream Came True

—eric—

next time you witness the triumph of love, do me a favor, and think of Mr. Valé. Five years ago Old Valé hobbled off into the sunset, cane in one hand, suitcase full of memories in the other. He didn't stay long, only long enough to never be forgotten. I still don't know what it was, but Old Valé had a way about him.

Most of them speak with a British accent and smell of pipe tobacco. But Valé didn't just speak; he sang every word, sounding a bit like Julio Iglesius would after dressing in angels' wings. Most of them arrive with an air of pomp and a nose lifted high. They are typically grumpy without even the decency to smile and shake your hand. But Mr. Valé was different. He stepped into my life with all the passion of a blindfolded schoolboy swinging at his first piñata. He slipped into my room and woke me with a belly laugh, grabbed his little Spanish guitar and serenaded me with the loudest and most sincere rendition of "Vamos a Celebrar" (Let's Celebrate) I've ever heard.

Most of them come and go, clock in, clock out, never to be remembered except for the mess they make and conveniently leave for their replacement to clean up. Valé came—not just to hang a token reminder of his existence on the coat hanger of time—but to change history—to put a dent so big that he could never be forgotten.

Valé loved life. He knew it was but a breath. So he came to spread glitter, slip extra cilantro into every chimichanga, blow kazoos, and make every kiss a little longer.

I knew the moment I first saw him that his time was short. He was aging quickly. But he wasn't going to let the fact that he was in his final hours deter him from squeezing life of all its zest. He had a job to do and nothing would stop him. His big blue eyes were full of radiant sunshine and seemed to say, "It's time, Eric!"

Valé had me laughing from the start. He also had me crying. I didn't do a lot of crying, but something about his tender love and inexpressible joy stirred me deeper than I had ever been stirred.

"Eric, you prayed for me to come, and I'm finally here!" His Spanish accent was full of gentleness and emotion. He kindly touched my chin and excitedly said, "In all your wildest dreams, did you ever think I would look like this?"

With a cry bubble in my throat and a tear welling in my eye, I spoke. "All I knew is that you would be worth waiting for. I just never would have dreamed that you would be so full of joy. You're perfect!"

After twenty-three years of dreaming and imagining what it must be like—watching it in movies, reading about it nearly every time I picked up a newspaper, magazine, or book—my Day arrived, sombrero and all.

I only spent a day with him—though he had been waiting since before I was born to throw me this great fiesta. God created Mr. Valé for one purpose. It was his life's work to decorate the stage for the most tender and precious of romances. He didn't just do his job well, he was the best I've ever seen. He was a better archer than Cupid and a better set-director than anyone in the history of Hollywood.

It was later that night, just before he passed away, that I saw him last. The guests had gone and I was carefully removing count-less grains of rice from my curly brown hair when he looked at me with reminiscing eyes and whispered in my ear.

"Amigo," he said softly, "God has given you something today that all the money in the world couldn't buy." With tears streaming down his aged cheeks he leaned down and kissed my forehead. "Never forget what God has done for you. And take good care of your princess." With that he turned to leave.

"Uh, wait," I said. "I don't even know your name!"

He paused and answered, "Oh, I'm sorry, didn't you know? I'm the Day A Dream Came True." With that he carefully placed his sombrero on his white head, picked up his cane and suitcase full of memories and headed for the door. But then before he strode off into the crimson night sky, he turned, and with that twinkle in his eye he yelled back, "But, Amigo, you can call me Valé la Pena."

"I'm sorry Sir, but I . . . I don't speak Spanish."

He let out one final laugh and then said with all the sweetness of a honey-drenched sopapilla, "My dear friend, it simply means, 'It's worth all the pain.'"

What a perfect name. For years I had waited for this Day. My Day of love; my Day of triumph; my Day of wedded bliss. There were countless times I thought I would never make it, but here I was watching my once in a lifetime Day fade into the night. A tear dripped from my eye and ventured down my cheek. What a Day it was!

"Thank you God!" I whispered with a smile forming on my moistened face. "I'll never forget . . . never!"

— awesome analogy

Little kids know how to dream. But as we grow up we quickly learn to be careful not to put too much stock in "happily ever after" conclusions. Once upon a time we innocently believed in fairy tale endings to difficult lives. But as we mature, and gain sophistication, we often stop believing in the Heaven at the end of the race, and so strangely dare only to believe in the hell in which we're struggling through today.

As one of my disillusioned and forlorn friends in college once said, "Hell seems very appealing right now, compared to what I have to look forward to in this life." When we experience disappointment we quickly run to the nearest rationalization to purchase a protective armor, so as to never let disappointment hurt us again. We stop living for something beautiful, and start accepting something mediocre.

In romance, we stop living for the "ride off into the sunset" endings, and start settling for "jerks-that-are-interested-in-only-one-thing" and flirts that only "want to feel special for a night."

The following story is our journey to find something beautiful in this world of disillusionment and pain. What we discovered can never be taken away, because what we found was hope. Hope in a world that misinformed us that we evolved from primordial slime and that God died with the polka back in 1960. What we found was peace. We found joy. We found a love that stared us in the eye and dared us to face the pain so as to gain the prize on the other side.

Well, Les and I found the pain that inevitably comes when you choose to walk a road-less-traveled—but we also found the prize. We found the troubles—but we also found the God who turns our troubles into glorious triumphs. We found loneliness—but we also discovered the wonder of sincere and tender relationships. Along the way we stumbled across an amazing secret . . . the secret to unlocking dreams.

Let this story offer you hope. Let it lift your chin and put a sparkle of vision back in your eyes and dreams of heaven back in your heart. Let God remind you how big He really is as—on a day when rice filled my hair and joy filled my heart—He reminded *me*.

Believe me. Ture love is worth all the pain that patience and perseverance can inflict. You'll have to experience it for yourself, but even something as simple as a kiss becomes unforgettable and priceless when the Author of Romance is scripting the love story. Let me tell you now—God is always near . . . *when dreams come true.*

Part One:

the search

Bittersweet Memories

-leslie-

a little girl with bright, sparkling eyes and long brown hair runs happily through the grass barefoot, wearing a flowing pink gown that used to be a lady's negligée. Now the billowing, lacy garment has been transformed into nothing less than a "princess" robe, filling this young girl's mind with glorious dreams and fantasies of far away castles and knights in shining armor. Suddenly she laughs, a pure sound of delight, and in her voice there is an innocence, a carefree, childlike spirit. Her name is Leslie. She is only eight. And to her, the world is full of endless possibilities.

a s the television screen displays our family home video, the frame wobbles to indicate that the videographer (a.k.a. my dad) is changing positions. I smile. My dad is a great sport. He never failed in his fatherly duty to either be busy with the video camera, the lawn mower, or the barbecue on hot summer Saturday afternoons.

The scene shifts and I catch a glimpse of two excited little boys, ages two and four, one in a cowboy hat and the other with an Indian head dress. The "camera man" struggles to keep them in the frame as they tirelessly bounce and squirm as only little boys can. Their hands and clothes are speckled with caked-on dirt and blotches of cherry flavored Kool-Aid as they fervently dig for worms and buried treasure in the plastic green turtle-shaped sandbox. And there is my mother holding their two empty "sippy cups" with plastic lids. One of the boys suddenly lets out a yelp of indignation, but before a battle can erupt, she gently bends down and, speaking in her calm, soothing tone, helps the grumbling cowboy and frustrated Indian make a peace treaty in only ten seconds. Then she notices the video camera and laughingly tries to motion it away.

I shake my head in wonder as I watch this vivid picture from the past that floods me with memories. Could I ever have been that young, that innocent, that carefree? Could I ever have known, as I floated through the grass in my pink satin gown, all the uncertainty and confusion that life would soon throw at me?

At eight years old, I knew without a doubt that someday my life would bring me a "happily ever after" ending. One of my favorite pastimes was sitting in our downstairs toy room on a bright yellow rug, listening with bated breath to various fairy tales (via my little orange Mattel record player) and following intently along with the brightly colored picture book that accompanied each romantic story. I had *Rapunzel, Cinderella,* and *Snow White* memorized and I was currently working on *Sleeping Beauty.* Without exception, every fairy tale ended with "happily ever after" and I was sure that someday mine would be no different. I was still young, but it didn't stop me from dreaming of my own prince charming

Not that my standards were high or anything! I simply looked at the men in my life to help me picture what a knight in shining armor was supposed to be like. First, there was my dad as handsome as any movie star on TV, stronger than the Incredible Hulk, wiser than the old Owl from Pooh Corner, and the most gentle and kind member of the male species my young eyes had ever beheld. He was everything I wanted in a man.

Then there was good ol' Ken, who always sat contentedly next to his gorgeous blonde date in her hot pink plastic Corvette while I zoomed them around my bedroom at full speed. Ken didn't say much, but his bright eyes and constant smile made a lasting impression on me. And if a girl as great as Barbie liked him, then so did I!

And lastly, I evaluated the heroes from my Mattel record player fairy tales. Gallant, noble, and brave, even in the face of ferocious dragons and vicious warlords. I knew I would never settle for less in a man. I wanted someone who was a combination of my dad, Ken, and Cinderella's Prince Charming. At the age of eight, I didn't think that was too much to ask. I knew he was out there somewhere. I knew someday he would rescue me at just the right moment and we would ride off together into the sunset. (Of course, I had also decided that my favorite dolls would be the guests of honor at our wedding and that my wonderful mommy and daddy would accompany my groom and I on our honeymoon!)

One night I had snuggled in between my parents on our mossy green couch to watch a movie. It was a love story. As it ended, I was less than impressed with the hero's qualities.

"He didn't even sweep her off her feet!" I complained loudly. "He's not good enough for her. I can't believe she settled for a guy like that!"

I still remember my dad's fond chuckle as he scooped me up into his arms and said, "Leslie, one thing's for sure . . . it's going to take a very special man to win your heart."

He had no idea how right he was. It wouldn't be too many years later that I would embark upon a journey to find true love. But the "happily ever after" ending I'd always imagined wasn't going to be as easy to come by as I once thought.

ah, memories in the form of wobbly home videos! Viewing them has become somewhat of a love-hate activity for me. I spend half the evening just trying to decipher the hastily scrawled handwriting on the label. I struggle to decide if the tape I'm holding contains Uncle Harold's fifty-sixth anniversary hay ride, or little David's two-and-a-half hour soccer game which was filmed so far from the field that all the players came out looking like little black dots. (Either of these two options could easily win the prize for America's Most Boring Home Videos.) Once I finally select a tape to watch, I am usually forced to spend another large chunk of time fast-forwarding through a TV special that my mom has accidentally recorded in the middle of the video. After enjoying a muted, high-speed version of *How the Grinch Stole Christmas* I finally arrive at little Johnny's space-ship-theme birthday party and realize this was not the video I wanted after all.

But there are moments when I stumble upon a scene from the past that grips my heart and floods me with emotion. As I watch little Leslie merrily dance around the backyard in her pigtails and bare feet, I experience such a moment.

I can almost smell the freshly cut grass and hear the shrill echoes of my little brothers' voices as they excitedly play out a duel to the death between their little green plastic army men. I can hear the distant tinkling music-box sound of the ice cream truck circling the subdivision, its high-pitched melody mingling with the dull hum of Mr. Harrison's weed-eater zapping loudly a block away.

I can feel the soft satin of my "princess" robe and remember for a moment what it felt like to be there . . . young and secure. I can imagine my dad teasing my mother, attempting to get her on camera. I can picture her shaking her head and laughter as she gestures wildly to him and turns her face away. All the fun and love that surrounded my childhood comes back to me in a rush. And as I sit here gazing at the television, I can only wonder . . . if I had known the road ahead, would I have taken those years of innocence for granted? Would I have clung to my childhood fairy tale dreams? I am suddenly filled with a desire to freeze the video screen and get that little girl's attention. I have an urgent longing to warn her . . .

Leslie, be careful with your innocence, guard it with everything within you. You can't understand now the cost of giving it away. Treasure your family. Cherish what God has given you. Hold on to your dreams. There will come a day when they will seem foolish. But they aren't. This world wants to steal your heart away and damage your precious innocence. But there's something more God has for you. Be careful. Please, be careful.

And yet I can't go back in time. I can't warn that innocent little girl of the traps that lie ahead and the romantic disillusionment that threatens to shatter her dreams. I can only remember back through the drama of my life—all the many moments, both good and bad, that were not captured on a video but were forever impressed upon my heart and mind. My fairy tale was a little more complicated than those entertaining stories on my Mattel record player. Yet the end goal was the same . . . a happily-ever-after story. But, like I said, it wasn't quite so simple.

I don't need a home video to remind me of every experience that shaped me or of all the valleys and the mountain tops along the way. I had a God who knew my every desire. He also knew how I would fall. And, yet, He was waiting on the other side of my failure and my shattered dreams with some dreams of His own . . .

Foothills High School

1987

-eric-

When most people think of education they think of chalk-boards, pop quizzes, boring lectures, and even spit wads. I think of lockers.

"Wham!"

That one single sound of dented and warped steel hammering against steel makes my skin crawl. Only the "bee-beep" of my alarm clock rouses a more insufferable memory.

There have been countless times when I have pressed my palms ferociously hard against my temples hoping to somehow squeeze out the memories associated with that abysmal sound of slamming metal.

But no matter how hard I press, I can't forget the *"Wham!"* Like a cat dragging in the smelly mouse and dropping it on the welcome mat, that *"Wham"* drags in all the memories from my childhood and plops them on the front doorstep of my mind.

The "Wham" reminds me of my education. Just like the lockers I slammed shut throughout my childhood, my true education was dented and warped. And that is not to criticize some of the wonderfully caring teachers I had growing up. I learned many quality things in the classroom. But my real education took place in the school hallway while leaning up against graffiti-laden steel with the number 215 painted on it. My *locker* was the potter's wheel of my young life. It was *there* I was molded.

"Hey Ludy!" the moist and sinful lips of Donny Lucero howled, "I'm a *bleepin'* fifteen up on you now, Dude!" (I use the term *bleep* instead of the actual cuss word since this story is an edited-for-general audiences rendition!)

When it came to locker talk, no one, and I mean no one, was better than Donny Lucero. And I should know, it seemed every school year his locker was always right next to mine. Lucero—Ludy. I think the alphabet was to blame.

"*Fifteen*, Dude!" He mocked, with a wicked twinkle in his eye, Lucero was always trying to coerce me into joining him in his manly pursuits.

You see, thanks to my tremendous education around lockers, I knew exactly what Donny was talking about. The translation into pure Christian book vernacular would be:

"Thou art a prudish monk, my dear foolish friend. For fifteen times I have fornicated with an easy maiden, and fifteen times I have experienced the essence of truest manhood. Yet you, O Ludy, are but still a little boy. When wilt thou ever become a true man?"

"Ludy!" I remember hearing as if it were yesterday. "Do you have any idea what you are missing?"

I didn't tell "Lucky" Lucero that I had never had sex with a girl. He just intrinsically knew. I wanted him to think I was a conqueror of the female species, but something about the way I lived gave away my innocence. Every once in a while I threw a cuss word into my speech to try and throw him off my trail, but it was as obvious as trying to spell the word "prude" with the letter "x"— it just didn't fit.

"Dude," I cringe as I remember saying, "I'm not missing anything!"

"Oh yeah?" Donny's beady black eyes grew enormous with interest. "Tell me Ludy, what was her name?"

"Uh, you wouldn't know her." I sputtered, my heart pounding with fear.

Donny drew close and carefully wrapped his muscular arm around my trembling shoulder. He smirked a devilish smirk, then with his practiced staccato voice said, "You might be surprised how many girls I know."

According to Donny's reputation I was surprised it was only fifteen. "Lucky" Lucero was Foothills High's definition of masculinity and I couldn't let him see me as the pure little Christian kid that I was.

"She doesn't go to school here," I lied. I could almost feel my nose hitting a growth spurt.

"I don't care where she goes, Dude. I just want the name of the girl that swooned in Ludy's arms."

"Uh," I floundered, "uh . . . Flarey," I mumbled, making up a name, sweat drops forming on my forehead. "Her name's Flarey."

"Dude!" He cheered and growled all in one breath while punching me in the shoulder. "Ludy, you're a stud!"

I know what it means to mess with dynamite while holding a burning match. Theoretically speaking, of course. At the age of sixteen, I desperately longed for something that I knew was dangerous.

All growing up, I heard the sermons on purity, the lectures about saving your virginity for your future spouse. I heard about the righteousness of God, and about the doom that awaited those who chose to defy Him. When sitting in a pew at church, surrounded by old people, it seemed pretty easy to remain a virgin. But standing at the lockers when Lucero was cackling in my ear about the thrill of a conquest . . . purity was simply an impossibility.

I didn't want to spend the rest of my life having to lie about some imaginary girl named Flarey. I wanted my own stories, I wanted to be able to brag like Donny. So somewhere in my teenage season of stupidity I made a choice to exchange purity for passion, and patience for predatorial behavior. "Lucky" Lucero was more than helpful in making the exchange as quick and as painless as possible.

"Eric, look at this piece of meat!" Donny's voice rose two octaves as he spoke and seemed to crescendo on the word "meat." Holding up a centerfold for my eyes to behold, he roared with pleasure, "Look at *her*, Dude."

I looked. Okay, I didn't just look, I *studied*, forging the picture of that young woman's body upon my mind forever. Whether or not the concept was ever spoken, I learned while shuffling through magazine pages that women were "objects" and not "people." If Donny had known the toxic and malevolent powers of the poison he was feeding me, he never once warned me. Someone might as well have taken out a pair of handcuffs and slipped them on me the moment my eyes first beheld a tattered *Playboy*. In fact, over the next decade of my life I often wished it was only handcuffs that held me to pornography. There is an easy solution to handcuffs—a key. This was an insipid sort of imprisonment. This form of imprisonment allowed me to think I was free so that I would never try to escape.

Every young man has a choice of who and what will mold him. When I was sixteen I chose Donny Lucero and his ear-tingling wisdom to be my Potter. I was never a handsomely-built love machine like "Lucky." Where conquest seemed natural for him, it was awkward and scary for me. My dad always taught me to treat a lady with dignity and sensitivity. In fact, he always used the words "delicate" and "fragile" when talking about my Mom. How could I forget a girl's feelings only to satisfy my own longings? Well, Donny assured me, it was satisfying *their* longings as well. They (meaning the conquered female) just didn't want to readily admit it.

"Lucky" spent his soul on hollow pleasures and never seemed to ache from the emptiness. Yet when I explored the very same hollow pleasures and ventured into the "forbidden," the flood gates of guilt were opened within *my* soul.

To me "Lucky" was just that—lucky. He didn't seem to have a conscience. He seemed to find fulfillment in following his baser instincts. He seemed to discover meaning and purpose in stealing from young ladies a treasure they didn't even know they had.

"Ludy?" Donny had shouted from down the hallway while I was getting ready to close my locker and head home for the weekend. "Dude, are you man enough for tomorrow night?"

"*Bleep* yeah!" I hollered in return, gulping as my conscience faithfully stabbed me with guilt.

My cheeks flush with anxiety; I rustled through my belongings to make sure I had everything I needed for the weekend. Satisfied, I zipped up my bag and, without even a thought, slammed my locker. "*Wham!*"

As I made my way through the maze of humanity toward the exit doors, I failed to realize that I was missing something. Something had slipped out of my possession and I hadn't even realized it was gone. I had lost my innocence.

Rutherford Elementary School
1987

-leslie-

i can't recall an exact moment when *my* innocence began to slip away. Nor can I remember a specific crisis point when I suddenly decided to turn my back on all that I once held dear. I think the change must have come gradually, almost undetectably, like the barely visible movement of the hour hand on a wall clock. I know that it started long before I ever reached the noisy hallways of slamming lockers where the hormone-crazed "Donny Luceros" lurked, hoping to add me to their list of "conquered females." It began when I was still a child.

As I began to approach the looming horizon of that uncertain place between childhood and womanhood, I can call to mind certain seeds of thought that were subtly sown into my young mind. Each seed by itself would have appeared harmless enough, but combined with all the other seeds, my childlike soul became polluted and confused. Looking back I realize that I should have recognized each of these finite seeds for what they truly were—tiny drops of poison slowly collecting to form a deadly venom. Yet for whatever reason, I allowed each tiny morsel to pass unchecked into the cavern of my heart, and then to leave its mark.

One of the earliest of these seeds of thought was sown during my sixth grade year, a tumultuous period of time I will never forget.

As a bubbly, outgoing fifth grader in my childhood hometown I'd had friends, I was accepted and liked, and I had been free to be a little girl. I traded stickers at slumber parties with friends, read Nancy Drew books, played the lead angel in the kid's musical at church, and wore my straight brown hair in pigtails. I took voice lessons and began writing songs—simplistic and childish, yet a reflection of the purity I still possessed. I would sing my songs to anyone who was willing to listen. I had no fear of what others thought. I was confident.

When I entered sixth grade after moving to a strange new town, things suddenly, abruptly changed. As I walked into the classroom on the first day of school with plastic barrettes in my hair and heart stickers on my pink notebook, I could feel the haughty disdain and hear soft snickers from the other girls who were meticulously inspecting my appearance. I soon learned that my days of carefree childhood bliss were over.

Each day became a constant struggle to live up to their standards so as not to be mocked or rejected. I began to dress differently, act differently, talk differently in order to blend in. The stabbing, brutal pain of their insults was more than I could handle. The entire first week of school I had sat alone, self-consciously chewing my nails as I leaned against a cold brick wall during recess. I enviously watched clusters of kids laugh and scream as they played various games. I glanced toward two or three small circles of giggling girls, who merely gazed back at me with snobbish pity.

Somehow over the course of that year, I learned how to live up to the standards of what was acceptable. In sixth grade, "fitting in" wasn't complicated—just wear the right clothes and have the right friends. That year, I was forced to switch to silver hair clips, start painting my nails, ditch Nancy Drew books, and abstain from collecting stickers. And for all my sacrifices I did manage to make a few friends. Inside I was lonely and confused about life, yet the childhood innocence was still intact. In the privacy of my own room, I still wrote pure songs of praise to my Lord. I still treasured my family and allowed myself to be an innocent child while at home.

But if I could have seen into my soul, I would have known it was suspended precariously over the edge of an ominous precipice.

The enemy of my soul must have noticed what I didn't see. I was vulnerable, and it was the perfect time to set the first of the poisonous seeds in front of me to see if I would bite.

i can still clearly picture Ms. Ashton. She was a stylish, silver-haired woman with a no-nonsense expression written all over her perfectly made-up face. She was the head of the counseling department at Westside Middle School—the exciting world all of us sixth-graders were bound for the following school year—and she had a mission. She had been invited to share with us about the wonderful, upcoming phenomenon we were all about to experience . . . *ad-o-les-cence*. She pronounced each syllable of the strange word as if hoping to somehow make our little brains comprehend the magnitude and importance of this vital information that she had been commissioned to share with us.

Ms. Ashton had a solemn dignity about her. She managed to command respect from her large audience made up entirely of wiggly eleven and twelve-year-olds, who would have snorted and giggled obnoxiously during a lecture on this particular topic had the speaker been less self-assured.

I can't recall the entire lecture, but the memory of that day is still fresh. As Ms. Ashton placed a detailed, scientific chart on the overhead projector and tapped each point about *ad-o-les-cence* with her long shapely fingernails, a stab of hopelessness overcame me. I felt like a doctor had just informed me in a matter-of-fact way that I was about to be struck with an odd disease. It was a sickness that would cause me to lose all reason and self-control, go through disgusting bodily changes, and spend several years of my life wallowing in helpless confusion. *Ad-o-les-cence* sounded like a horrifying time of life . . . not the wonderful and "special" experience Ms. Ashton promised it would be.

But more than creating the subtle dread of *ad-o-les-cence*, there was something else Ms. Ashton fed my mind that would come back to haunt me for years.

"I know, boys and girls, that you've all been warned about the risks of experimenting with drugs, alcohol and sex," she told us crisply. "However, I am not ignorant of the fact that before you leave middle school, *each and every one of you* will have experimented with at least one of these three activities." She paused and eyed us smugly while her shocking "statistic" slowly made its way into our brains. Then she ended the topic with unwavering finality, "Just be sure, kids, that when you *do* experiment . . . you do it *safely*."

I swallowed hard at her words. Drugs, sex and alcohol were the three big "no-nos" I'd heard about for nearly my entire life as a young Christian. I'd made a decision long ago that no matter what the temptation, I would make it through my teenage years abstaining completely from all three of those "no-nos".

But now came a moment of doubt. More than anything, this difficult year of my life had awakened the unquenchable longing to "fit in," to be "normal." To somehow, some way, avoid the stinging remarks and jeers of haughty peers who didn't like me. If what Ms. Aston said was true—that *everyone* was going to experiment with the very activities that went against what I believed— what kind of grief would my commitment cause me in the years to come? A creeping insecurity about what I believed began to grow in my heart. Would I miss out on a normal growing up experience just because I was the only one with certain standards?

I was too young then to know that the three "no-nos"—drugs, sex and alcohol, were only a small part of the forces that would fight to steal away my innocence over the coming years.

I didn't decide at that moment to compromise my standards or sacrifice what I believed for the sake of "fitting in." Like I said, the change came so slowly I hardly noticed it. But that unforgettable lecture from Ms. Ashton had planted deep doubt. As if on cue—according to her scientific chart—I did precisely what she and others encouraged me to do as a pre-adolescent . . . I began to question everything I once believed.

Mountaintop Christian Camp
1988

-eric-

You man enough, Milo?" My devious eyes poked at my good friend's pride as I motioned with my pointer finger toward an unknown redhead innocently chattering with her girlfriends. "Tell her you love her, dude, just walk right up to her and announce the simple truth."

"No way!" groaned Milo Richards, his bushy eyebrows furrowed in disgust.

"Come on, dude!" pleaded scrawny little Pete Blakely who was drinking in the sunshine and attempting to flex his tricep muscle for a flock of girls who had just traipsed by. "She looks ditzy—she'd probably like a guy like you, Milo."

In response to Pete's audacity, Milo ground his knuckles into Blakely's bony chest until the cry "Mercy!" was heard across the teenage populated lawn.

The grass was freshly cut and the air was filled with the thrill of "the hunt." And "the Dudes" were checking out all the new possibilities.

"Whoa!" Jimmy Cowels howled. "Three o'clock, aqua blue shorts!"

"She's mine!" cheered Bobby Gilbert, the teenage equivalent of Tom Cruise.

"I'm the one that saw her, dude!" Jimmy argued, knowing his rights as an un-chartered member of "the Dudes" were limited—seeing as how he just unofficially joined last Monday.

Jimmy needed to learn that Bobby was the kingpin. And it was an unspoken rule that he always got first pick. He was the *true* womanizer. The rest of us were wanna-bes hanging out in his shadow, attempting to reap the benefits of his reputation.

As soon-to-be-seniors, "the lawn"—nestled right smack in the middle of the rustic campground—was *our* domain. This was our last year of camp eligibility, so we all felt an urgency to enjoy it to the utmost. Subconsciously we felt every girl that providentially happened to attend Mountaintop this summer was ours to either claim or toss aside.

"Here she comes, Dude!" I howled with excitement and nudged Bobby in the ribs.

I was great at motivating shallow love affairs. I knew how to say things like, "You man enough?" or "Come on Dude, you scared?" Saying those things made me feel a little like Donny Lucero. The problem was, I didn't like it when anyone said those things to *me*. Because I *wasn't* man enough, and yes, I *was* scared to death.

As the gaggle of young ladies naively approached the starving lions in their den, Bobby once again proved to "the Dudes" why he was a *true* womanizer and why the rest of us would always remain wanna-bes He had guts!

"Hey!" he boomed with a deep bassy voice and a little nod of his stubbly chin.

"Hi!" the heavily perfumed crowd giggled in return.

A sudden realization flooded each and every "Dude's" mind.

That's Brad Bink's baby sister!

"Uh . . . uh . . . uh!" Bobby floundered.

There was an unspoken rule amongst "the Dudes." I don't know who officially drafted it, or how it evolved, but it was one of the biggees. "Dudes don't date little girls still in puberty." This rule ranked right up there with "use the word 'dude' at least three times in every sentence" and "never admit, even under severe torture, that you spent a Friday night babysitting your little brother."

As Brad Binks' baby sister stood giggling with her eighth grade horde of puberty-stricken adolescents, Bobby tried desperately to gracefully exit from this blunder he had unknowingly waltzed into. And I learned why *not* having guts could *also* be a blessing.

———

y parents had applauded my maturity when I announced I was headed for Mountaintop Christian camp the summer of 1988. I knew that when my parents heard the word "Christian" they would smile and think lofty thoughts of their seventeen-year-old son.

Maybe we've been reading Eric wrong, Honey. Maybe, just maybe, he does have a heart in pursuit of God.

My heart aches as I think about my motivations when I was seventeen. The Christian youth culture I grew up in knew how to fool the "parent" generation. All we had to do was put the word "Christian" in front of whatever we did and it made even the most devious of activities sound virtuous.

Like the time I told my mom that all my "Christian" friends were getting together for pizza and I needed five dollars. My mom warned me that too much pizza would only exacerbate my pimple-problem, but she finally—after much maternal huffing and puffing—reached inside her purse for the five big ones. After all, it was a "Christian" get-together.

Well, the pizza wasn't the only thing that five dollars was used for that unforgettable evening. That robust summer night, my friends had a surprise awaiting their innocent Eric Ludy—whom they dearly loved to see slide down the cliff of compromise right next to them. My Mom thought I was cavorting with "Christians." And I guess in a way I was. As the stripper removed her clothes, and my heart and mind turned another shade of black, my friends and I were living out our own version of "Christianity"—sainthood on Sunday, and hypocrisy and compromise the rest of the week.

" ric, dear!" My mom had said as I was heading out the door to my car, my backpack slung over my shoulder with all of my camp necessities inside. "I'm just so glad you chose to take a week and spend it focusing on Jesus."

"Uhmph." was my predictable response as I turned the door handle, eager for my escape.

"Mommy!" my obnoxious little brother, Marky, blurted, "He's going for the girls *not* God!"

Leave it to a stinkin' little brother to blow my cover. Brothers inherently know the sins of their siblings even before they are committed. But I was a master at the art of acting the "perfect Christian young man."

"This is a *Christian* camp, Marky!" I said in my sweetest most angelic voice while snarling down at my devious little brother.

"Eric," my mom whipped out her maternal lecture. "I want you to know that God is working in your life in ways that you can't even see right now." She moved in and tenderly wrapped her soft arms around my neck.

I instinctively pulled away from the show of affection.

"Just know," she gently whispered as if she could see right through my tough exterior and straight into the insecurities hidden within my heart, "God knows the *real* Eric Ludy. And He loves him so much!" Then as she squeezed my neck the way only a mother can, she said, "and so do I!"

My parents had always told me to lead instead of follow the crowd. They had told me to shine the light of truth within the darkened world in which I lived. But there was a reality that they must *not* have realized—the world doesn't want to hear about Jesus.

My youth pastor had told me that being a Christian was "cool." Well, that seemed to be true during youth group and at home, but it sure wasn't true everywhere else I hung out   I just knew that God wouldn't have wanted me to live in such a way that people mocked and ridiculed me. After all, wasn't popularity a tool that I could use to lead friends to camps like Mountaintop where they could hear the Gospel and be saved? Both Peter and Jimmy were at Mountaintop the summer of 88' because I told them about how great it was. Okay, I didn't tell them about the boring Christian stuff they were going to hear. I just subtly mentioned that the ratio of girls to guys was two-to-one and that all of them were drop dead gorgeous.

———

ten minutes, guys!" Our faithful leader chanted as he ran by our patch of "the lawn."

"Ten minutes to what?" Bobby yelled out in grave disappointment. He knew that two in the afternoon didn't mean "dinner time." It could only mean one thing . . . .

"Chapel!" the muscular messenger yelled from the distance as he continued on his crusade to let everyone be properly informed.

Chapel. The one blemish on teenage Christian summer camps. Chapel to Bobby, Milo, and me was a necessary evil. It was chapel that assured our conservative Christian parents that we would spend one week of our lives force-fed truth, and therefore chapel was the secret ingredient to getting our parents' stamp of approval on our week of "girls, girls, girls."

"*Bleep!*" Bobby cursed. His lips curled in outrage.

"Are you allowed to say that here?" Pete asked in all seriousness.

"*Bleep* yeah!" Bobby pompously stated. "I can say whatever I *bleepin'* feel like!"

"What's chapel?" Jimmy inquired of me with a twinge of annoyance in his voice.

"Ah," I fumbled. "They're just gonna talk to us and tell us things about God and stuff."

Boy was that awkward! Something about Christianity embarrassed me and I felt like if they associated me with this whacko religion, I would completely lose their respect. So I added, "It just sort of goes with the camp."

Jesus was only a cuss word to Pete and Jimmy. And I was afraid to let them hear about Him as anything else. Maybe because Jesus was very little more than that to *me*.

How important could God possibly have been to me if I was willing to disassociate myself with Him to secure my reputation with two skinny little greasy haired seventeen-year-olds. I wanted my friends to see me the way I saw Donny Lucero—as a ladies man. And Jesus Christ seemed to smack of weakness and purity, not the pompous brawn and perversion I wanted to emanate.

Ironically, Pete and Jimmy were deeply impacted by chapel. While Milo, Bobby, and I squirmed around, whispered in each other's ears, and checked out the July inventory of cute female campers, Pete and Jimmy focused intently on the speaker.

By the time our week of frivolity was through, amazingly both Pete and Jimmy had given their lives to Jesus Christ. But their new-

eric

found faith didn't last much longer than the bus ride home and through the remaining weeks leading up to the start of our senior year. And I'm afraid now that I know why.

For Milo, Bobby, and me, Christianity was a duty. We put up with it because we wanted to go to Heaven when we died. We attended Sunday school and went to youth group not because we *wanted* to, but because it was a requirement of a Christian teenager who wanted to have a peaceful home life. We wanted others to accept Jesus, but it was more so that we wouldn't feel as abnormal than that we truly longed for them to find salvation.

When Pete and Jimmy came to Jesus, they looked around for real life pictures of what it meant to be a Christian. And unfortunately they saw *us*. They saw three young men, paying our dues to the God of the Universe by acting out the "good little Christian" at the appropriate and safe times during the week, and then living like everybody else every other moment.

The culture I grew up in excused and allowed Christianity if it was packaged nicely in a dusty old book and stayed there. You could announce that you were a Christian and no one cared. You just weren't allowed to live it. The moment you gave even the slightest glimmer of Jesus in the way you lived, mockery and ridicule awaited you with its fangs of rejection ready to bite.

I learned how to please the culture in which I lived. And, amazingly, I felt no guilt. Because all the other Christian young people I knew were living just like me. There was definitely not the slightest concern that anyone could possibly ever think that Jesus Christ was more than just a cuss word in my life.

Lakeshore City Church

-leslie-

Pounding metallic music vibrated with deafening volume as small clusters of teens and pre-teens began to congregate in the youth room on Sunday night. Some headed straight to the orange and green garage sale couches that were scattered throughout the room, others made a beeline for the pinball machines and video games. Flirting couples teased and chased each other around the room, occasionally collapsing into a breathless tickling match on the floor. Girls sat possessively on their boyfriends' laps, while others whispered juicy tidbits of gossip into each other's ears. I hesitantly entered the room just as our good-looking youth pastor, Kevin Richards, stood up and began waving his tanned muscular arms to get everybody's attention.

"Yo, people! Listen up! Time for 'devos' okay?" he boomed in his expertly polished California-surfer accent.

Though I had only been attending youth group for a few short months, I had already learned that the word "devo" was our youth pastor's "cool" way of referring to a devotional time. After about five more minutes of chaos, he finally managed to get the stereo turned off and herd the group of about fifty hyper adolescents to the chairs in the front of the room.

"Okay, people," he continued in a more normal tone of voice as he smacked loudly on a piece of gum and ran a hand through his shock of "male calendar model" blonde curls. "I've got, like, a couple announcements . . . this Friday is the *Holy Mayhem* concert at Michaels' Arena downtown. Be at the bus with your tickets by, like, seven, okay?" A few enthusiastic cheers echoed around the room.

"And," he went on, "Saturday is our awesome lock-in at the high school gym. Bring your sleeping bags and, like, some junk food." He paused and looked out at us with a mischievous sparkle in his blue eyes. "We're gonna PAR-TY!" This got him a wild applause from the entire group.

When the noise had subsided, Kevin sat down on a stool and faced us. His expression became serious and he took a deep breath to signal that he was about to begin that night's "devo."

"I want you guys to realize," he began sincerely, "that I *understand* where you are at in life. I know that, like, not a single one of you in this room is, like, actually getting along with your parents."

My mouth opened slightly in surprise as he looked around at us knowingly.

"In fact," he added in a challenging tone, "if anyone in here can say with complete honesty that you actually *like* to be with your parents . . . raise your hand now."

A quiet hush fell over the group of about fifty young people as we gazed back at the trendy clothing and bronzed physique of our twenty-two-year-old youth pastor. My heart began to pound as not a single one of my peers raised their hand. But the truth was, *I* could have raised *my* hand. *I* loved my parents. I loved spending time with them. At the confusing age of thirteen, I valued their support and encouragement and advice. I met Kevin's probing gaze and he lifted a questioning eyebrow as if to say, "So . . . you want to contradict me?"

It was a moment of crisis. I knew what I should do—raise my hand and prove that being a teenager doesn't *always* mean you have to hate your parents. I wanted to argue that he was wrong—that I loved my parents, that I enjoyed spending time with them and that they were my closest friends. But then I remembered the peers around me—guys mumbling perverted jokes to each other or staring at the floor with bored expressions, the girls whispering bits of gossip in each others' ears and glancing haughtily around the room at their rivals. This was not a benign group. If I were to raise my hand and challenge the words of our ever-cool, highly esteemed studly leader, Kevin . . . I would be mocked. I would be patronized. I would be attacked.

I pursed my lips together and kept my hand down. After several heavy seconds of awkward silence, Kevin went on with his speech. "Just as I thought," he remarked with a sly grin. "*No one* in here has a good relationship with their parents. Now since I know that to be true, I want you all to know that during this time of your life when you can't, like, relate to mom and dad anymore . . . *I'm* here. Hey, I'm young and I can *relate* to what you're going through. I mean, your parents haven't been in high school since, like, before the Dark Ages. Let's be real here, your parents are, like, kind-of . . . out of it, you know?" Kevin's voice held a hint of conspiratorial mocking, and he seemed pleased as a few sincere heart-felt murmurs of agreement from the girls and mumbled comments like "right on, man!" from the guys rumbled around the youth room.

—

Confusion swirled around in my mind as I hurried out of the youth room that fateful night. According to Kevin, now that I was thirteen, I was supposed to start hating my parents. *What is wrong with me? Why am I not normal? Maybe I really am the only one in that entire group who could have raised my hand. I'm sure that if I had told them all the truth—that I still really love to be with my parents, I would have looked like the biggest idiot. Maybe Kevin is right—maybe something is wrong with me if I like my parents. After all, he's a Christian youth pastor!!*

With all my heart I wanted to be accepted, to simply "blend in", to go through *ad-o-les-cence* as normally as I possibly could. Yet, it seemed from all angles and directions, who I was and what I had always known was being challenged . . . and pulled away from me. I had been a Christian since I was five years old. I had Christian friends. I went to a Christian youth group with a Christian youth pastor. And yet, even in this "spiritual" environment, a place where my faith was supposed to be nurtured and strengthened, I felt the very foundation of all the ideals and values that my parents had invested in me over the years, being ruthlessly stripped away. I didn't know what to believe anymore.

That night, and for many nights to come, my quest to be normal seemed like the most important thing in the world. I was so caught up trying to decide how society expected me to think and act I simply didn't hear the still small voice that was trying to warn me . . . "Leslie, don't listen to these voices of confusion. Hold fast to what you believe. Don't sacrifice your innocence. Don't try to be like them . . . you'll regret it if you do."

Instead, I accepted the tiny poisonous seed from Kevin Richards, the confident young leader. I allowed it to creep into my mind and take root. And it wouldn't be long before I started reaping what I had sown.

The Ludy Dinner Table
1989

-eric-

i may have learned about "manhood" while leaning against my locker, but I learned how to be disrespectful and disharmonious while leaning my elbows on the Ludy dinner table.

"Join our family circle." Old reliable spoke. His predictable words were as familiar as "hello" and "goodbye" to us hungry Ludys. In response to my dad's gentle request, we all joined hands and bowed our heads. Since I was sitting next to Marky, I offered him my pointer finger to hold. It was my older brother way of saying he wasn't worthy of my entire hand.

"Father," my dad reverently prayed, "we thank You for Your many blessings." As my dad continued, Marky brushed the back of my hand against the slimy butter dish. A swift kick from my right foot to his shin was his just-reward for his impudence.

"Owww!" was the exaggerated noise that issued forth from his little brother larynx.

My dad, who was very used to such interruptions continued on until the word "Amen" was muttered by all Ludys.

We all simultaneously lifted our heads, bracing ourselves for the upcoming battle. My mom's eyes perused the northeast corner of the table where the horrible sound of suffering had been heard. Krissy carefully reached for the peas and Daddy prepared his napkin on his lap. Marky and I just groaned.

"Boys!" My mother's searching glare was cutting and unrelenting as her voice crescendoed on the "oys."

"He kicked me!" Marky howled.

"He got butter all over my hand!" I moaned.

"Eric Ludy!" My mom chanted in her corrective tone. "If you want us to treat you like an adult then I suggest you begin to act like one!"

"Why are you only looking at me?" I pleaded. "He got butter all over my hand!"

My parents didn't allow me to speak so rudely, but after studying how my friends talked to their parents, I guess I felt it was necessary to follow in the footsteps of the rest of my generation and put parents back in their place.

"Eric!" My dad chimed in, his face still calm. "Don't talk to your mother like that."

I had been grounded a thousand times and spanked what seemed like *ten* thousand times throughout my strong-willed childhood. But as an eighteen-year-old high school graduate, my parents were not willing to resort to a wooden spoon to correct me anymore. They had come to the place where the only thing they could do was pray.

Like all my other friends, I had learned how to distance myself from family. I had my own car and could escape the house at will. I had plenty of activities during the week that kept me occupied and far away from the "oddballs" of my life.

I had a weird family and I didn't want the rest of society associating me with them. Krissy, my older sister, had chosen radical Christianity over popularity. In high school she had chosen to befriend all the "losers." She didn't realize *my* brilliant theory, that you can't lead people to Jesus if you don't first of all have a measure of popularity. Marky and I mockingly referred to her as "the Saint." She sincerely seemed to love the whole "God thing," and I had to classify her as "extreme"—otherwise I would be admitting that I, as a fellow Christian, was supposed to be like her—*weird!*

Marky, my loathsome little brother, was personally responsible for securing me over five hundred spankings growing up. As a little brother there were certain rules he needed to abide by, and he broke every one of them. Rule number one: Never make your big brother—who can beat you up—look bad in public. Well, I was convinced that he broke that one just by calling himself a Ludy. He also severely transgressed when he, being two-and-a-half years younger, started shaving the same year I did. I also considered the fact that he weighed more than me and looked older than me an unforgivable mistake.

Rule number two: Don't ever bring discomfort of any kind to your brother, who has power to make your life very uncomfortable in return. Well, in a nutshell, he broke this rule so many times growing up, that I had, by the age of eighteen, run out of creative forms of little brother torture. You see Marky, to *me*, wasn't a "human" with dignity and value. He was a *brother*, designed by God to be picked on, criticized, and laughed at.

Affection was a big thing in the Ludy household. We were, and still are, a huggy family. At any moment a tear could be shed and a hug given. After spending eighteen years as a Ludy, I was used to it. I didn't like it, but I was used to it. There was only one person that I refused to be huggy with. Little brothers would see a hug as a sign of weakness. Marky, as far as I was concerned, would never find my arms wrapped around his Polo drenched body.

Daddy was the easiest Ludy for me to deal with. Probably because we didn't talk very often. Except for his little chat with me when I was thirteen about the Birds and the Bees, the only thing we ever discussed was the Denver Broncos. He was a traveling dad, always on the road bringing in the bucks. Provision was his means of telling us how much he cared. At eighteen, I would never have admitted it, but I wanted my Dad to be there for me. I probably would have pushed him away, but I secretly wished he would have wrapped his strong arms around me during one of my teenage tirades and whispered, "I love you!" My mom knew how to express how she felt about us kids. But as a guy, I needed to hear it from my dad too.

Mommy and I were like oil and water. Once my body clock struck twelve, my mom and I just couldn't relate to each other. What she thought was fun I thought was boring. What I thought was fun she thought was "a compromise to my Christian witness."

She was always inviting people into our home. Strange people! People that, I felt, belonged in a place that smelled more like *them*. She was always sharing about Jesus. Jesus, Jesus, Jesus! She never tired. There were times I would come home from school and a homeless person would be sacked out on my bed. I was embarrassed by my mom. Other moms were cool. They allowed their teens to do whatever they wanted. My mom always had a curfew, a restraint, a limitation to tack onto my already difficult life.

I'll never forget when Mike, a caustic and perverted senior, asked me if I was a religious nut like my mom. With a knot in my throat and a knife-like pain in my conscience, I had confidently replied, "No way!" My response still haunts me. It reminds me how far I have since come.

My family was something I put up with. I endured them for the sake of security. The very same group of people I used to laugh with, cry with, and enjoy spending all my time with when I was ten, were now housemates that reminded me of the purity I once had. I guess that is why I pushed them away.

a re you kids packed for the reunion?" My dad excitedly asked as we dined on my mom's scrumptious chicken enchilada casserole.

"I still need to do one more load of wash," Krissy angelically proclaimed.

"I'll get packed tomorrow night." Marky offered.

"But, Mark dear!" Mommy noted. "We're leaving the next morning!"

"It will only take me two minutes!" He passionately reasoned.

All eyes turned to me. I was still wiping butter from the back of my right hand. "What?" I said with a snarl on my lip.

"Are you packed?" My mom repeated the question for the remedial student.

"Uh, . . ." I moaned, took a deep breath, and mumbled, "I don't wanna go!"

Shock and bewilderment filled the Ludy kitchen like a dense fog.

"You . . . *what?*" My mom carefully reconstructed my outrageous decree.

"I said," gaining steam, "I don't wanna go!"

My mom's eyes sent an urgent message to my dad that he better do something, *and quick.*

"Hold on, Eric," he boomed. "What makes you think this is an optional trip? We have always gone to the reunion as a family."

"Til' now!" I barked.

"What would you plan on doing? Staying home alone?" My mom's voice was more pleading than corrective.

"Yeah!" I proudly agreed. "It would be great to be alone."

"Well, what would you do?" My dad remonstrated. "You just quit your job for the remainder of the summer."

"I want to be with my friends."

Oh, how I wish I could rewind my life back to this moment and say something different. Even as I remember it tears come to my eyes. Without even a thought about the pain I had the power to inflict with the words of my mouth, I spoke. And my words were like a knife. This ~~little group of four, as odd as they were, were my life.~~ ~~They were the ones who would stand by me through thick and thin.~~ ~~They were the ones who would love me even when I was unlovable.~~ And it was this little group of four that I stabbed. I simply said, "I want to be with my friends." Reunions were a family tradition. Those were my family's fondest memories. But *I* chose my "friends." For years to come the pain from that little episode around the Ludy dinner table remained. Thank you God, for second chances.

311 Rambling Rose Road
1988

—leslie—

now that you're thirteen and in junior high school, Leslie, we want to start going through this workbook with you," my mother informed me as I sat across from my parents in our living room.

I lifted a skeptical eyebrow and gave her a less-than-enthused expression as I studied the two teenagers on the front cover of the book. Their clothes and hairstyles were twenty years behind the times, and they stood happily with their beaming parents underneath the bold red title, *My Journey Through Adolescence*. I sighed.

"Nice outfits," I commented sarcastically as I studied the cover with the best "bored out of my mind" expression I could muster. My mom gave me a warning look and opened to the first page. I knew it was useless to argue against the idea. My parents were determined that "open communication" was something we all needed to focus on, especially now that I was a "teenager." Recently I had glimpsed certain new books on their bedside table with titles like *How to Talk to Your Teenager* or *Surviving the Terrible Teens*. I knew they felt they were losing touch with me. And they were right.

I had always been able to come to my parents about any problem or concern. But now, something was different. Something held me back from opening up to them about what was really going on in my life.

Deep down, I was well aware that the real reason I was so reluctant to go through a "workbook" with my mom and dad was something far deeper than the ridiculous-looking cover or dorky title. I knew that *My Journey Through Adolescence*, as out-of-touch with modern times it may be, would still force my parents and me to discuss topics that I would rather have avoided . . . like school, friends, peer pressure, and sexual temptation. They would probe, ask questions about what was going on in my life. And right now I just wasn't sure if I really wanted them to know.

I had also recognized the author's name on the workbook—a well-known Christian leader. Bringing my Christian faith into these discussions made the whole situation even worse. It would serve only to remind me how lackluster my relationship with God had become over the past few months. A stab of guilt pierced my heart . . . how could I possibly be pulling away from Him, the One I had loved with all my heart since I was five years old? And yet, somehow I knew that was exactly what I'd been doing—pulling away from God just as I had pulled away from my parents.

As these thoughts swept like a tidal wave through my conscience, I mindlessly followed along as my dad quietly read the first section aloud. I didn't pay close attention until we reached the part I had been dreading . . . the discussion questions. I made an effort to tune in to the conversation just in time to realize my mom was asking me the first question . . .

"Do you have any examples of peer-pressure situations you've faced at school lately?" They both raised their heads from the page and looked at me expectantly as I bit my lower lip and pondered how to reply.

Peer pressure situations? I thought to myself ironically. A better question would have been, "Do you ever have any moment during the day when your eyes, ears and conscience aren't being assaulted and attacked by every form of evil and perversion?"

I summoned up a mind's eye view of a five-minute period in the hallways of my junior high school. I could hear the metallic "wham" of lockers slamming shut echoing through the corridors, adding to the roar of chaos and confusion as hundreds of teenaged bodies ran, pushed, and shoved their way through the halls. I could hear the screams, shrieks, and giggles of flirtatious girls scampering away from greasy-haired boys laughing wickedly as they chased any member of the female species in sight with the goal of touching them in a sexual way. I could remember the foul language swirling around me as kids cussed out their teachers, their parents, and each other. I could hear the perverted jokes and the wild laughter of boys who stood huddled at each other's lockers, drooling over pornography. I could see the little plastic pink container that Susie smugly showed me during math class . . . it was filled with little bags of white powder.

What could I tell my parents about this world? How could they ever understand? Avoiding peer pressure? It was a little more like walking into hell everyday and attempting to somehow come out unscathed.

"Leslie?" my dad prodded, and I realized they were still waiting for an answer.

"Um, I really can't think of anything right now," I finally mumbled.

Glancing at each other in mild frustration at my vague response, they moved ahead to discussion question number two: "What are some ways you can prepare now for the sexual temptation that will come as you get older and start dating?"

I looked away from their steady gaze as they waited for me to participate in the conversation. When I didn't appear to have anything to add, they began to share some ideas.

"It's important to know what you believe about sexual temptation before you start dating," my dad told me. "You need to make sure you only go out with Christian young men who believe in saving sex for marriage—just like you do. Then you won't be forced to end a relationship over that issue."

"You should think of responses ahead of time," added my mom, "so that if someone approaches you to have sex with them, you will already have thought out how to say 'no' in the best way possible."

I chewed on my lower lip thoughtfully as they spoke. It's not that their suggestions weren't good—but they kept talking about sexual temptation as if it was somewhere down the road of my future. I didn't know how to explain to them that I already faced it nearly everyday.

My thoughts drifted to the conversation I'd had with Bryan, a studly fifteen-year-old soccer player whom I'd met at the mall with my friends. He'd been calling me for about two days, "just to chat"— or so I thought. But last night as I'd held the phone to one ear and fiddled with my math homework he had asked me a question that had jarred me into reality.

"So Leslie, I want to ask you something. I know we both are really attracted to each other so I just want to get right down to it . . . when do you think we can have sex?"

I was speechless as my yellow pencil dropped onto the glass desktop with a loud thud. I knew I should have called him a slimy little pervert and slammed down the phone, never to speak to him again. But instead, I had simply stammered out the words, "Um, can we talk about this later, Bryan? My mom's calling me for dinner," leaving the issue unresolved—and leaving the door still open for the highly hormonally-motivated Bryan.

I knew that eventually, before he started putting too much pressure on me to have sex, I'd have to break things off with Bryan. I felt strangely disappointed. I had been insecure for months about my physical appearance, and it was actually flattering to at least have someone who "liked me" that I could giggle with my friends about. I would never have broken my commitment to sexual purity just to hold on to Bryan—but I realized that if this was all most guys were after, the next few years of my life were going to be desperately lonely. I wondered despairingly if, once word got around that I was a "prude," any guy would ever want to ask me out again.

Bryan's proposition wasn't the only problem I'd had with "sexual temptation" in the past months. At school I was constantly around guys whose minds and mouths were from somewhere even worse than the gutter. To fit in socially, I learned that I was expected to carelessly subject myself to their disgusting sexual jokes and comments, and that if they tried to grab or touch me in the halls— which happened regularly -I was supposed to act as if I thought it was funny . . . even invite it.

As this reality whirled around in my mind like a ruthless tornado, I began to resent the fact that my parents were not even close to touching the reality of my world. I had concluded that they really were clueless about my life . . . and I had no way to explain it to them.

I don't remember exactly how that conversation continued, but it ended with me yelling at them, "You just don't understand! You'll never understand!" and running tearfully up to my bedroom to slam the door. I threw myself across my bed and sobbed miserably, feeling like I was being swallowed up by an endless black hole.

I hadn't wanted to believe I could ever lose my closeness with my parents. But Kevin Richards, the studly youth pastor, had been right after all. It had happened even to me. As much as I didn't want to admit it to myself, they simply didn't understand me anymore. And something told me this wasn't a problem that was going to disappear anytime soon.

t he life of a thirteen-year-old girl is highly melodramatic. Whether the issue at hand was which color of nail polish to wear to the school dance or what posters to hang in my bedroom, there is one theme I remember from this time in my life . . . *everything* was a BIG DEAL.

It's true that I sobbed as if my life were over anytime I had a remotely embarrassing experience. Like when I wore high heels for the first time to a nice restaurant with my sixth grade friends and slipped down a spiral staircase with a plateful of steaming food in front of a crowd of gawkers. And I won't deny that I begged my mom to let me stay home from school whenever I had a bad hair day. In light of my rather tumultuous emotional state back then, it would be a temptation to assume that I over-evaluated the pressures I faced at this time in my life. Maybe it was just hormonal changes. Maybe I was just over reacting. Maybe things weren't as bad at school as I remember.

And yet, maybe they *were*. In fact, maybe they were *worse*. In spite of all the usual teenage struggles, I can't forget the deeper, much more intense battle I faced internally. The feelings of hopelessness, emptiness, and despair that surrounded me during that time are just as real now as they were then. I had an enemy. And he was working overtime to destroy me at that young, impressionable age. I don't believe I exaggerate when I say this . . . his plan nearly worked.

The loving, trusting companionship I'd always had with my parents was stripped away. My two little brothers—my favorite childhood playmates—hardly saw me anymore. My faith in God was weakening. My daily time in prayer and seeking Him was almost nothing. My leaders at church—like my youth pastor Kevin—were not only failing to lead me closer to the truth, they were actually warping my perspective—doing more harm than good. My friends were shallow, gossipy, and selfish. And behind it all was the driving, intense passion to be liked and accepted and normal.

Though I wasn't a loner or a reject in junior high, neither was I considered "popular." I felt like I was always hanging on the fringe of the in-crowd, never quite sure what to say or do to fit in. More than once, I had been the brunt of cruel jokes and ridicule by my peers. There was a daily competition to put each other down as low as was humanly possible. And there were constantly people—mostly pimply-faced, greasy-haired boys with obnoxiously squeaky voices—who were on the hunt for an easy target. They seemed to sense my delicate uncertainty and vulnerability and pounce on it.

For no paticular reason they would make fun of my clothes and my looks and erupt into wild, inhuman laughter as I tried to act like it didn't bother me.

"Just ignore them, Leslie and they'll go away," had been my mother's words of wisdom. It wasn't that easy. They would throw books or pop cans at me, or surround me so that I was helpless to escape. In my mind, I knew that the reason they were so merciless to me was not because I was ugly or idiotic, but because they were sure to get a reaction. But my heart didn't believe this truth. I felt worthless as they teased me. As hard as I tried, I could not seem to keep the humiliation off my face at their harsh words. It was torturous.

At the very time in my life I wanted to feel attractive to the opposite sex, it was implied that no member of the male gender would ever find me remotely desirable. Foolishly, I chose to believe what a small group of pathetically ridiculous specimens of humanity told me about myself, and I was left with insecurity so overwhelming I often cried myself to sleep at night in sheer agony. Somewhere in that horrible year of my life, I made a commitment to myself. I looked ahead to the upcoming years and decided there was only one way to survive . . . obtain popularity at all costs.

If I have to make it through six more years of this kind of hell, I remember thinking, *I will do whatever it takes to make sure I at least have popularity. If I'm going to survive, I have to be liked. I have to somehow become attractive to the opposite sex. It's the only way I can make it.*

I had been a little girl once, full of romantic dreams, full of innocent bliss. I had imagined a fairy tale love story. I had pictured a handsome, caring, and tender man coming into my life at the perfect moment. I had longed to be a radiant, beautiful princess who would be loved and cherished forever by the man of my dreams. I had carried those hopes with me even into my early teen years. Yet all it took was that one hellish year of my life and my dreams of a perfect love story crumbled and faded like smoldering ashes. Prince Charming didn't exist. There were only boys trying desperately to act like men, and failing miserably. They were boys who had no concept of love—they simply acted out animalistic drives. If this was all there was, I didn't want to dream anymore. All I wanted to do was survive.

I had even briefly considered the idea of sitting down with my parents and trying to make them understand my world. Maybe I could try to express my heart through writing a song. I quickly pushed aside that thought. It was hopeless. Even if I could somehow convey the horror of what I had to face everyday . . . I had a nagging fear that they would embarrass me somehow—maybe even force me to leave school. I pictured my friends always remembering me as "that girl who had to leave because she just couldn't take the pressure." I sighed helplessly.

There was always that still small voice cautioning me otherwise. It tugged at my heart to remind me that this was not how God wanted me to live. But I was tired . . . too tired to listen to that little voice any more.

Baldwin Hall

Spring Semester, 1990

-eric-

f or years I had dreamed of getting away. Going to college "in-state" wasn't even an option. I wanted to make my own way in life, blaze a trail without somebody telling me how to blaze it. I wanted to go somewhere Ludys weren't known. A place where my reputation was like wet concrete. I could start wearing a baseball cap and make that my new symbol. I could get good grades and fool everyone up at college into thinking I was an intellectual. I wanted to make a change. Little did I know what type of change I would be making.

To my parents' delight I chose a Christian college. But sometimes what you find hidden behind the word "Christian" is anything but.

"Ludy," the pointy-nosed Eleanor Radcliff challenged. "It's a well known fact that the Bible is a collection of myths and legends." A grunt of agreement was heard around my smelly dorm room from the other members of our informal college "discussion" group.

"Yeah! There's even a guy in it that supposedly lived over nine hundred years!" added Eugene Belz with a snort of disbelief.

"Exactly!" Eleanor cheered, smirking with approval at Eugene, her new-found debate partner. "Historically it has always been weak-minded and weak-willed people who assume the Bible to be handed down from some god in the clouds!"

"I think the Bible has a lot of good ideas in it," chimed in our resident redhead named Rudy Compton.

"I think it has a lot of great ethical concepts," Eleanor aceded without a moment lost, "*but*, so do many other religious books." Then after letting out a ponderous sigh, she stated, "I just believe it shouldn't be put up on the pedestal that Ludy over here wants to put it!"

All ten of the visiting eyes in my dorm room turned and looked at me with interest. My entire life had been lived without any philosophical or theological challenge. The people I hung out with in church growing up didn't know how to put two thoughts together in a griddle and scramble them, let alone defend their position against the likes of Eleanor Radcliff.

"Uh, . . ." I passionately argued, "uh, . . ."

"Ludy?" Eleanor went in for the kill. "Do you even know why you believe what you believe?" The hint of sarcasm in her voice was like Novocaine to my brain—I was intellectually paralyzed.

"Uh, . . ." I continued with all the passion of a wounded turtle. "I just think it's the truth."

My cogent logic was overwhelming for this group of "brains." So much so that they were forced to roll their eyes and change the subject.

<hr/>

eleanor Radcliff was my first taste of spiritual reality. For the first time in my life, I was being seriously challenged to examine my belief system. Donny Lucero and his cronies never questioned what I believed; they just wanted to make sure I eased their consciences by compromising along with them. Milo and Bobby never challenged my Christianity. In fact, brainlessness *was* our version of Christianity. Maybe Eleanor was right. Maybe I was one of the weak-minded and weak-willed idiots she was referring to.

<hr/>

i t was January. I was a fresh nineteen, full of energy, full of passion, and full of questions. For the nearly two decades I had walked this earth, I had been zealous. I passionately identified with the ideals I held—the Denver Broncos being the best football team in the world, Canadian bacon and pineapple being the toppings of choice for the true pizza lover, and of course, Steve Perry being the ultimate male vocalist in the universe. For nineteen years I had frothed at the mouth in defense of what I believed. But what I defended wasn't eternal. It was hollow and meaningless. For the first time I began to wonder about things that really mattered. Life, death, my purpose here on this earth. I began to question everything I had ever held true. Who was Jesus anyway? He could have just been a great man, like Eleanor said. What if He wasn't God in the flesh? What if He *didn't* rise from the dead, like Rudy believed? What if my parents had been wrong? An emptiness and hollowness filled my heart even as I pondered the possibility. What *was* Truth anyway?

I remember glancing up toward my bookshelf as I lay prostrate on my bed. There jammed between my Genetics and Organic Chemistry manuals was hidden a book. Three weeks ago I had slipped that book onto my bookshelf more to bolster the impressiveness of my meager library than as a potential source of reading material. I had purposely forgotten about it. But in a strange and mysterious way it was reminding me of its presence, and I couldn't seem to ignore it.

Three weeks prior I had excitedly arrived back at college from Christmas break. It had been wonderful to see my family again, eat the home-cooked meals, and most of all, sleep in. But something had gnawed at me the entire snow-laden month. *Was my family wrong? Could Eleanor Radcliff possibly be right?*

Christmas morning had been chock full of joy and memories— and one very awkward moment. My sister Krissy gave me a gift. The fact that she gave me a gift was not unusual. It was *what* she gave me that caused the discomfort.

Krissy was known for her eccentricities. She had chosen a missionary school over college. Where every normal graduate seeks out a high paying profession, Krissy seemed to seek out how poor she could become for God. To me, everything she did was extreme. She even *prayed* about what she should give as a Christmas present to her younger brother, Eric.

"Oh . . . it's a book!"

I smiled on the outside and thoroughly wondered on the inside as to the mental competence of my older sister.

She should know, darn good and well, that I don't read.

Not that I couldn't read. I just didn't like reading. My brain seemed to spit out anything I read except for the *Sporting News, Sports Illustrated,* the sports page, and the mandatory textbook reading I had for college.

Even though it was obvious I would never read such a stupid book, all she had to say for herself was, "Eric, I think you're gonna like it."

Now as I lay on my bed in my dank dorm room, this crazy Christmas gift was announcing its presence. The book might as well have been glowing. I knew I needed to read it.

Why did she give me a book? She knows I don't like books!

There was a knowing deep down that this dusty book on my shelf held an answer for my searching heart. My sister might have been different than other people, but she had something in her possession that I longed to have as well. She had peace, joy, and purpose. I didn't want to live life all radical and weird like she did, but I at least wanted to find out what she knew—that I for some reason was missing.

At nineteen I didn't comprehend the power that was working in my life. I didn't see that a sovereign hand was directing my steps, even

eric

when I thought *I* was making all my own decisions. All these years later, it is transparently obvious what God was doing. *He was speaking to me.* Not in an audible voice, but in a way that transcends my understanding—even now. All I know is, a gentle voice was communicating with my heart.

As I flipped open the cover of my sister's present, I was awestruck by what I began to read. It was the story of a man whose life goal was to find the Truth. He looked everywhere for it . . . Eastern religions, various cults, different mysticisms. I found myself on a journey with him, asking questions in sync with his own. *Why? How? Where are you God?* Until one day on his incredible journey . . . *he found it!*

Almost like waking up from a dream, my eyes opened and a whole new reality came to life. My heart was pounding and my palms were sweaty as I felt an intense longing within my heart to accept this man's discovery as my very own. I could hear Eleanor and Rudy's questions begging for my attention, *"How can you believe in something, Ludy, that you can't prove in a laboratory?" "Do you know for sure that an all-pervasive truth even exists?"* But those very questions that had haunted me over the past few months now seemed like infantile rationalizations in contrast to the overwhelming and obvious Truth I was now grappling with.

"Jesus!" I stammered, "Jesus!"

My eyes blurred with salty tears and my heart ached with remorse. I found myself on my knees, struggling to find a position that would acknowledge the presence of the Almighty God of the Universe.

I had spent my lifetime accepting Jesus Christ as a means of salvation. But this fateful night, He was suddenly infinitely more. I had spoken His name thousands of times growing up, but now His name meant something wonderful to me. I was seeing more than a talisman of hope in the person of Jesus. I was seeing a real historical figure who lived and breathed just like me. But He was different. He was God. *And He was ALIVE!*

"Jesus!" I pleaded. "Forgive me!"

Something beautiful was taking place inside of me. It was almost as if a gentle hand placed a blanket of hope around my shoulders, tender lips kissed my cheek with an unquenchable love, and I was drinking a bottomless mug full of indescribable peace and joy.

I had known Jesus Christ my entire life. But not like this man in the book knew Him. This man, who was strangely like me—strong-willed, blunt, and egotistical—one day encountered Jesus. He realized that Jesus gave up *everything* for him, and now the *least* he could do would be to give *everything*, including *his life*, back to Jesus. It was suddenly so simple. Life had a purpose. Life had meaning. And God was near. Maybe He had always been near, but now I recognized His closeness and discerned His infinite power that held the universe in place.

Eleanor and Rudy's wisdom seemed like a little ant challenging a hippo to a fight. Everywhere I looked, the very way God created things seemed to give backbone to the truth of Jesus Christ. I had to do what the man in the book did.

"Jesus?" I cried. "Take my life! Do with it whatever You please."

I let go . . . and I was forever changed.

I reached for the white phone on my desk. I carefully picked it up, my hand trembling, my heart thumping. I found the list of "important phone numbers" that my mom had made for me when my parents dropped me off at the start of the school year. My eyes scrolled down until I found the one I was looking for. I slowly pushed the numbers—then waited with bated breath.

"Hello!" came the sweet voice on the other end of the line.

Silence. I didn't know what to say.

"Hello?" the angelic voice again questioned.

My voice just wouldn't work. I cleared my throat and with great emotion I finally spoke.

"Ah . . . Krissy?"

There was a long meaningful pause and then my sister finally spoke.

"Eric?"

"Uh, . . ." I let out a deep breath and struggled to continue. "Krissy? Do you remember that book you gave me for Christmas?"

I paused while fidgeting with my Bic pen and struggling to find the right verbiage to express what I was feeling inside. Krissy patiently awaited my words.

"Well, . . . I read it." There was another long silence as I attempted to overcome the cry bubble in my throat. "Krissy, I gave my life to Jesus."

There are certain moments in my life that I can never forget. This was one of them. After years of praying for her little brother. After years of mockery and the pain of being misunderstood. And after years of hoping her big little brother would one day realize the true Source of life . . . Krissy received the phone call. There wasn't anything she could say . . . all she could do was cry.

Ridgeview High School

1990

-leslie-

i leaned against my bright red locker, tightly hugging a stack of textbooks to my chest and listening to the buzz of conversation swirling through the air from the noisy huddle of girls surrounding me. They were all talking at once, but I was used to such moments . . . in fact, I lived for such moments. Instead of being on the outside fringe of this group as had once been the case, I was now the focus of their attention. Putting on my best "poised and confident" act, I laughed with them and added witty comments at the right points in the conversation. I had learned a lot over the past two years.

"Oh, here he comes, Leslie!" Kelly squealed, and all eyes turned to gaze worshipfully at Brandon Wood's tanned physique and blonde hair as he strutted over to us with a small smirk on his face.

"You are sooo lucky to have him, Leslie," Amanda crooned to a chorus of murmured agreement. "He is so adorable!"

The warning bell suddenly blared and the energetic group of females dispersed.

"See you in fifth!" Kelly sang over her shoulder as she bounced away, her cheerleaders' skirt swaying dramatically with each step.

"Bye!" I answered as I turned to smile up at my boyfriend of five months. He was grinning sheepishly, hiding something behind his back. The pace of my heart quickened and I raised my eyebrows expectantly.

"Happy five-month anniversary," Brandon whispered lovingly as he presented me with a full red rose wrapped delicately in crackly green tissue paper. My eyes sparkled with emotion as I carefully took the gift.

"Thanks," I answered softly, brushing my lips against his. He pulled me closer and kissed me again. For a moment time stopped as we stared into each other's eyes with passionate longing. Then the final bell shrieked rudely and we broke away to make a mad dash for our classrooms.

———

my interaction with Brandon wasn't always this picturesque. He was fifteen, I was fourteen, and we were attempting to have an adult relationship. Most of the time I felt like a little kid pretending to be in a soap opera. Brandon had been a perfect find. He was just the type of guy I had always been told I was supposed to look for—a nice, solid Christian young man who shared my commitment to abstinence. It didn't hurt that he was also good-looking, popular, and an amazing athlete. Since I'd first started "going out" with Brandon (toward the end of my eighth-grade year), I had been accepted into the world of popularity and suddenly had more friends than I could keep up with. The pain and insecurity of my early junior high school days were finally buried under the whirlwind of my newfound social world.

Life was better—or so I told myself. I made sure I kept preoccupied enough with dances, parties, friends, and my wardrobe that I didn't have to think about the fact that things weren't really as great as they appeared.

At home, my relationship with my parents was still distant and strained. In fact, I had even stooped to lying to them about where I went and what I did when I was out with my friends.

It had started one night when I'd gone to a movie with a bunch of "friends"—which was actually Brandon and another dating couple.

Brandon and I sat in the back of the movie theater for the entire night—entangled in each other's arms and passionately making out. Before we left the theater, I ran to the bathroom to check my appearance.

"Oh no!" I gasped in horror as I caught sight of a bright purple mark on my neck, glaringly noticeable against my fair skin. My heart pounded as I turned the top of my turtleneck up, but I breathed a sigh of relief when I realized it covered the incriminating evidence of my activities.

When I arrived home that evening, I held my breath as my parents casually questioned me about the movie and who I had been with. I answered their interrogations as vaguely as possible. I was sure that any moment they were going to guess what I had done. But soon they made their way upstairs to go to bed, unsuspecting of my inner turmoil. I escaped to my room and leaned hard against the door as I closed my eyes with relief. But the feeling was short-lived. I was soon weighed down by a huge flood of guilt. *How could I have just looked them in the face and lied to them? They trusted me!*

Trying to ignore my smarting conscience, I fell asleep that night vowing to myself that I would never lie to them again. But I soon found out that this lie was to be just the first of many more over the following months—and each time it got a little bit easier. Each time the stab of guilt was a little less sharp.

There were moments I wished I could run to my parents and tell them everything. I hated myself for who I had become. I had no time for what was truly important in life. God seemed as far away as ever. I still called myself a Christian and went to church, but my lifestyle only indicated that my passion was to achieve and maintain popularity. Yet everything I did—I told myself during these irritating moments of guilt—I did only to survive.

Popularity was not all I had hoped for. It was a constant rat race, a competition, an all-consuming mission to become someone I was not. My popular friends were mostly shallow, gossipy, manipulative and two-faced—either back-stabbing or kissing-up depending on the situation. It took a great deal of energy to keep and maintain good standing in these friendships. But in my mind, it was worth the effort. Popularity was my only shield of protection in a world of darkness and merciless cruelty.

Though I wouldn't have admitted it out loud, I knew that my relationship with Brandon was the main reason I had so many friends. Which is why I was determined to hold on to him no matter what. And that wasn't always easy.

It wasn't that Brandon didn't *want* to be in a relationship with me. In fact, sometimes he was so possessive of my time that I felt smothered. He insisted that we talk on the phone for at least two hours every night. On weekends, he would call me as soon as he woke up, even before getting out of bed. He waited for me after almost every class. He brought me a rose on each month-anniversary that passed. He had started telling me that he loved me only a month after we had started dating. (I say dating, because that's really what it was—although I was not officially allowed to "date" yet. I somehow found ways around my parents' rules.)

Every time Brandon said the words "I love you," I felt obligated to say them back. It became a habit we practiced several times a day. But it didn't feel right. I knew that I didn't love him, that I really was too young to even understand that kind of love. I felt guilty somehow, saying something so deep and meaningful when we had no lasting commitment to back it up. I knew I could never marry Brandon. He was a Christian, yes, but like me, his life was all about self-promotion. He was certainly not the tender, sensitive, Prince Charming of my childhood dreams. He wasn't the kind of man I could spend the rest of my life with. But for now, he was all I had.

There was another problem. The physical side of our relationship was a constant source of confusion. By the time I was fourteen, the majority of my friends were having sex with their boyfriends. It was no secret. In fact, when I would get together with a group of girls often the juicy details of their sex lives were the subject of our conversation. Most of them probably assumed I was having sex with Brandon, because I never told them differently. They had also observed how physically affectionate I was with him in the hallways, at school, and at parties. But Brandon and I had agreed not to have sex because, as Christians, we knew it wasn't right until marriage.

I had remembered the advice of my youth leaders and parents from years earlier. "Before you begin a relationship with someone, decide together where you are going to draw the line physically and stick to it."

I think Brandon and I had half-heartedly drawn *our* "line" at kissing and hugging.

But in dark corners of parties or movie theaters—when couples all around us were entwined in fits of feverish passion—that "line" didn't hold much weight. The standard for our physical relationship quickly lowered to the point of doing almost everything—except technically breaking our commitment to abstinence. *This is not the way a Christian is supposed to live,* a little voice inside would chastise me whenever I found myself in a dark room on Brandon's lap, allowing his hands to explore at liberty.

But there was always a justification for my actions, not the least of which were the unforgettable words of my trusted youth pastor, Kevin Richards . . .

O kay, people, tonight our 'devo' is about love, sex and dating," he announced one Wednesday as the hyper group of young people settled down more quickly than usual. During that talk we all had one question on our minds. It was articulated best by Jason Watson, a burly, sixteen-year-old football player.

"Yeah, man, I was just wondering," he stammered awkwardly as all eyes rested upon his red face. "I mean, I know that sex before marriage is wrong and everything, but like, I mean . . . how far is too far? How far can we go before we're 'sinning'?"

How far is too far? This was the infamous question burning in the heart of every shallow Christian young person attempting to ride the fence. We wanted to hang out as much as possible in the "gray" territory when it came to right and wrong. It was certainly burning in *my* heart. I leaned forward intently as Kevin smiled confidently and rose to the occasion. I never forgot his answer.

"Well, Jason, that's a good question. I mean, do you guys really think that God is like, hanging out in Heaven, ready to strike you dead with lightning the second you come close to messing up? No man! No way! God knows we're only human! He gives us the Holy Spirit to convict us and guide us. Now, the answer to your question 'how far is too far' isn't in the Bible. But here's a piece of wisdom for you guys. When you're with your girlfriend or boyfriend and things start to get a little hot, just go to the point where you feel comfortable, then stop. Hey, if you're still a virgin, then you're obeying what God says! So don't get all hung up about the gray areas. Just trust Him."

I was still a virgin, and according to Kevin Richards, I was justified before God in my actions. I convinced myself that I was being faithful to my future husband simply because I was committed to "saving sex for marriage." But deep down, I knew better. And yet since the biggest spiritual leader in my life told me it was okay, I used it to justify what I did with Brandon.

More than anything I wanted to hold on to Brandon and the popularity he brought. As our relationship continued, there were times his smothering affection became frightening. But whenever I started pulling away from him, emotionally or physically, he became unglued, angry, and depressed. We had plenty of fights over this issue. I wanted more freedom and time with my friends, he wanted more of my complete attention and affection.

Then, about eight months into this complicated relationship, Brandon realized that he had become somewhat of a sex symbol at Ridgeview High School. He noticed that he was much-in-demand by many available and beautiful young women. I wasn't giving him what he desired—total and complete devotion. I wasn't having sex with him.

I remember that I actually started to feel bad for him—that he made the 'sacrifice' of being with me when he could have gone out with plenty of girls who would have had sex with him many times over. *I* had been the one to talk Brandon into a commitment of abstinence, and I was fairly certain he would have tossed this commitment out the window, had I not been so determined to "wait." I tried to make up for it by giving him even more physical passion by lowering the standard as much as I possibly could. But it was no use. The more I gave away physically, the more I felt dirty and used. Brandon was growing more distant as he realized that there were other fish in his sea. I knew the end of our relationship was near.

Part of me felt relieved because I had been so drained from trying to keep him happy yet maintain all my other friends—not to mention my grades and other activities. But the bigger part of me was in sheer panic, because for nearly a year Brandon had been my identity, my source of popularity, my security. He had been the hand I held as I walked into a room full of strangers. With him I felt beautiful and attractive and desired. And without him I didn't know how I could survive in my cruel world.

I will never forget the night we broke up. It was probably one of the most traumatic experiences of my life—even to this day. I knew it was time. We just couldn't get along anymore. I knew I couldn't be the kind of girlfriend he had grown to desire. I had seen his flirtatious gaze resting hungrily on other girls lately—girls who flirted back with open invitation. When his back was turned they would glance at me with sneering haughtiness as if to remind me that Brandon no longer worshiped the ground I walked on. I couldn't handle the gut-wrenching pain of rejection I felt during those moments. So I became moody and distant toward him. He couldn't deal with me anymore. It was over. We would still be friends, we said. Yeah, right.

I remember throwing myself across my bed, my body racked with heartbroken sobs that shook me to the core. My mother tried to comfort me, but I felt like something inside had died. It was like someone had taken my delicate heart and fragile emotions and ripped them out and shattered them all over the ground into a million pieces.

My security was gone. I didn't know who I was anymore. I didn't care. I didn't even want to live. The thought of going to school the next day and facing the triumphant, haughty gazes of girls who were once my friends, was more than I could handle.

I was so upset that I actually made myself sick and I didn't go to school the next day. I walked around in a daze, mechanically forcing myself to breathe in and out.

When I showed up at school two days later, things were as I had expected. I walked down the crowded hallways alone and tried to ignore the snickers and whispers that followed me like a looming storm.

"Isn't that Brandon's old girlfriend? Didn't he like, dump her for someone else?"

"Yeah, I don't know why he stayed with her for so long. She's not even that cute. She looks like a snob."

They made sure their words were spoken just loud enough to fall on my ears as I passed by. Then they would smirk at me with lips curled in an expression of mock pity and disgust. My stomach was so tied in knots that it was weeks before I had an appetite again.

This horrendous experience was far worse than the ridicule of the junior high boys from two years earlier. It was the most cutting pain I had ever known. But it wasn't just the biting comments that hurt. I knew I had lost something precious in the process of my relationship with Brandon. I had given away the deepest part of me to someone who no longer appreciated it, no longer wanted it.

I saw Brandon a few times in the hall that week. Our eyes met, but we both quickly looked away. He had stolen something from me—my very heart. And now we were strangers. Less than two weeks later, he had selected another girlfriend. My last clear memory of Brandon was watching from a discreet distance as he stood near her locker and tenderly gave her a beautiful red rose wrapped in crackly green tissue paper. She reached up to kiss him. And *he* put his arms around her. I felt sick and ran to the bathroom.

The next few months passed in a blur. If I had been lonely and insecure as a skinny, brace-faced thirteen-year-old in the seventh grade, I was doubly so now as my popularity hung shakily on the edge of a weakening cliff. And I simply didn't have the emotional energy anymore to try to maintain it.

In desperation, I looked for other relationships. I had a few flings with guys I didn't care about. No matter how I truly felt about them, I tried to summon up enough energy to pour myself completely into each relationship—my heart, my emotions, my physical affection. I hoped to somehow keep their desire for me strong. But nothing lasted. Every time it came to that unavoidable place of "breaking up" I braced myself for that familiar devastation. My heart had become a mass of shattered pieces. I simply didn't care anymore. The standards I'd always had for myself as a Christian didn't seem to matter much anymore—though somehow I still attempted to cling to the last remaining remnant of my virginity.

I longed for the pain to go away. I became like an addict—compromising myself physically and emotionally with guys I barely knew and was not even attracted to, only to wake up the next day feeling sick with remorse and the powerlessness to stop myself. I lived life in the fast lane of an American high school girl's dream. But I had taken the turns a little too sharply, and now my life had finally spun out of control.

I maintained a few friendships that year. I still went to dances and parties and football games. And somehow I still managed to cling to a dwindling thread of my popularity. But inside there was nothing. I was only numb. My music was the only outlet of expression I had—and all my songs were dark and despairing.

I don't remember everything clearly. But I know it was the lowest point of my life. A few fleeting scenes enter my mind of the way I became during that time. I see a girl with the right clothes and the right looks, but a girl with hollow eyes and a hardened, bitter smile. I became a master in the art of flirting and seduction, a master of the haughty attitude, the gossiping, the lying, and the filthy language. I am still haunted by the songs I shouldn't have listened to, the jokes I shouldn't have laughed at, the movies I shouldn't have watched. I didn't compromise in these areas just once in a while—it was nearly every hour of every day. Looking back, it all runs together like a nightmarish dream. But I know it happened.

And amazingly, through it all, there was a God watching me fall, watching me break His heart, and loving me still . . . .

Stewart Hall

Fall Semester, 1990

—eric—

1 ife was brand new. Sunsets were rosier, grass was greener, and even girls were prettier. But I was determined to change my ways when it came to women. I mean, I was a new man. I wanted friendship first. I'd heard an older Christian single say that he was focused on "friendship first" so I thought I'd choose the higher road too. No longer was I a Donny Lucero or Bobby Gilbert wanna-be. *I was the new Eric Ludy.*

I attempted to rationalize away the fact that my lips ended up plastered to Gretchen Smalley's outside my parents' house in my parked car last summer. *We were becoming friends! We talked about God! At least she was a Christian!* It seemed all my attempts to change my ways were proving only one thing—the old and the new Eric Ludy were both suckers for a flirtatious girl.

At the start of my sophomore year of college I was through with "my summer with Gretchen" and beginning to pray now about my love life. That was a very new step for me. Up to this point, I had never even considered talking to God about my relational life. Now I was praying things like, "God, I met a girl today. Maybe, if You think that it could be something more than friends, You could bless it?"

There was still a problem. I wasn't too interested in what God had to say about my choices. I just wanted His blessing. I was willing to discuss it with Him, I just didn't want any negative feedback. It was then that Laura LaTourno came waltzing into my world.

For the first time in my life I prayed from the beginning of a relationship to the end. Something like, "God bless this amazing relationship! Show me how to be a friend first. Help me to spend more of our time together talking about You than kissing and touching her."

What a prayer! I'm sure the angels who overheard my pleading were moved to tears.

Over the following months, I continued to pray, but I also continued to struggle. Laura and I went to Bible studies and prayer groups together, but all that spirituality didn't seem to rub off when her puppy-dog eyes searched mine. It was like I couldn't think straight when I turned on the romantic afterburners. I knew that what I was doing was wrong. But I felt like an alcoholic in a bar attempting not to sip the mug of whisky I was holding in my hand. I was an addict to sin.

My passions were driving my life. God was now supposedly the center of my existence. But why could I not live differently than I had before?

With an overwhelming sense of guilt and an all-consuming desire to draw a line of demarcation in the sand of my life, I parted ways with Laura. It was my way of rewinding life back to that fateful night I read the book and gave everything to God. It was a tearful and painful separation, but I knew that if we continued I would have been leading us both away from God.

Over the next couple of weeks, I tossed and turned in bed, I struggled with my studies, and was unable to focus in my classes. God was knocking on my heart. I desperately wanted to open up, but I just couldn't. I thought I had given Him everything that night ten months prior. I mean, it was true that my life had changed since that night—I was different. I was thinking about the needs of others, I was loving in a way I never had before, I had a joy and a peace that was real and beautiful. But there was something I hadn't realized that I was still holding on to.

Trust Me, Eric.

The knocking on my heart was nearly unbearable. Intellectually, I could understand allowing God to mold me into a humble, loving, compassionate man. But I couldn't comprehend letting go of that which I held most dear to my heart.

God, I want to trust, but I just can't!

I understood God healing my soul, providing for my needs, comforting me in times of suffering, but I couldn't comprehend Him taking control of this all-important area of my life and doing with it whatever He saw fit.

God, I've never heard of anyone giving that up to you! And I'm scared that if I do You will not manage it and take care of it the way I think You should.

As hard as it was to be honest with God, I sensed an incredible peace when I finally let down my spiritual facade and admitted my real struggle—I didn't think He had any clue about romance. If He took my love life into His hands I was afraid He would surely either destroy it or give me something less than lackluster.

Trust Me, Eric.

For weeks I struggled to pry open my hand and let go of my hold on the steering wheel of my love life. For weeks I tried to rationalize away such a radical decision. But for weeks, God pursued me like a hound dog after the wounded fowl.

I tossed in my bed at night, bleeding from all my mistakes with the opposite sex. I inwardly groaned as I thought about how poorly I had made decisions. And one clear truth seemed to run across my mind like an electronic message board:

Eric, you'll only be ready to relate to a member of the opposite sex after you get to know Me, the Creator of the opposite sex.

I knew He was right! I had to fall in love with Him before I could ever comprehend how to be a true lover. If I ever expected a match made in heaven, I had to give Him the pen to write my love story. I had to let Him design my romantic life if I truly desired to be unhindered in my love relationship with *Him*.

"God, I'm willing to let You have Your way!" The words flowed haltingly from my lips. My head was buried in my arms. I was all alone in my dorm room, but it seemed all Heaven was keenly observing.

There were three things stirring within my heart. And I knew I needed to enunciate each of them for all the heavens to hear. With a knot in my throat I carefully spoke the first.

"I'm willing to be s . . . s . . . single!"

I knew I was holding on to my right to be married. And I knew God needed to have total control to do whatever He pleased, even if that meant *He* was my only love for the rest of my days on this earth.

Feeling the weight of my every word I continued with a thumping heart and moist hands.

"If You desire marriage for me, I will trust You to pick her out."

I was scared as I gave God the right to choose. I didn't know if he would find the same things to be beautiful that I did. What if He couldn't tell the difference between a twenty-year-old girl and a one-hundred-and-three-year-old widow?

I stood up from my chair and got down on my knees. I knew what I was about to say, and I felt I needed a more reverential position to utter the words. With hands outstretched toward something unseen, I swallowed hard and spoke.

"The next girl I date God, . . . will be my wife!"

Evergreen Christian Camp

1991

—leslie—

What am I doing here? I wondered dully as I shifted in the uncomfortable folding chair and attempted to concentrate on the speaker's boring lecture. I glanced furtively around me at the hundreds of teenaged bodies sandwiched into the stifling auditorium. There was not one familiar face among the whole group. I swallowed back a huge, discouraged sigh as I realized I still had eight days left of this "good experience"—as my parents had prophesied my time here would be. I felt agitated and restless. I was so used to filling every spare second of my life with frenzied social activity. With a wry smile, I realized this was probably because I was addicted to my little world of friends—it was all I knew, all I had to cling to. And maintaining my world of friends created just enough chaos in my life to cover up the emptiness I felt inside.

Evergreen wasn't exactly a camp. It was more like a training school, designed to prepare Christian high schoolers for what they would face in college. I was only fifteen, younger than most of the attendees, and I can't say I was interested in the hours of lecturing I was subjected to each day. I wasn't in the mood for making friends. I wasn't in the mood for anything. I felt despondent. During free time I joined in conversations half-heartedly, then found myself wandering off alone, basking in the bright mountain sun and trying to sort through my cumbersome emotions.

"Hey, Leslie," Abby Johnston's Texas accent broke into my somber reflections one afternoon. I smiled at her weakly.

"So, mind if I join ya'?" she drawled while carefully sliding up onto the large boulder I had claimed as my spot for the day.

"Sure, go ahead," I replied a little late. There was an awkward pause as we studied the valley miles below us.

"Um, so, how are you liking it so far?" I finally asked, feeling the need to create small talk. Abby's eyes shone as she scanned the spectacular view.

"I love it here, Leslie!" she sighed happily. "God is doing so much in my life! I mean, being in the mountains and seeing His majestic creation an' all! I've just been reminded how much He loves me!"

I studied her profile as she spoke. The wind gently lifted a tendril of hair away from her kind face. Abby was not a beautiful girl. I could tell from her simple clothes and unassuming manner that she wasn't a popularity queen either. It's not that she was ugly—she was just kind of plain looking. She probably didn't have guys calling her every night. She probably hadn't even gone to prom or homecoming (the worst fate that could befall a high school girl as far as I was concerned). I wondered how she handled life without friends and boys and parties. It sounded hollow and depressing. But there was also something in Abby's eyes that fascinated me. She was peaceful. She was content. And I knew her life had meaning.

A stab of regret coursed through me as I suddenly realized that this simple girl named Abby had a living, daily, active relationship with the Creator of the universe. *I had that once*, I told myself inwardly. *But I don't feel like I even know Him anymore.*

Throughout my earlier years, I had always been the girl with the quiet confidence and inner peace. I had been the one to tell all my friends about the amazing power of God's love. And even during high school, even during the lowest points in my life, I was still "closer to God" than most of my friends. To the outsider, I was still a good, moral, Christian kid. I had mastered the art of "riding the fence,"

leslie

maintaining a spiritual side by attending church and youth group yet secretly living a different life at school and weekend parties.

But now, watching Abby's eyes sparkle with love for her Lord, I realized what I had lost. I had not been living the life of a true Christian. I had left my first love—Jesus Christ—and followed after my own desires. And now my life was empty. My heart ached for the next two days as I methodically went through the motions of the camp routine. I could feel an inexplicable pull on my spirit—and I eventually realized where it was coming from. God was calling me back to Himself.

Finally, on the last night of camp, His still, small voice got through to me. I felt a rush of emotion well up inside of me at an alarming rate, and I knew I needed to be alone, and pour out my heart to Him. I rushed away to a quiet place and dropped to my knees, tears spilling down my cheeks unnoticed. ·

"Oh God, forgive me," I cried out in anguish. "Forgive me for pulling away from You. Forgive me for throwing away my innocence. Forgive me for rejecting my wonderful family. Oh, Lord, I want to change. I want to escape the death-grip of the popularity trap, but I don't know how. Please help me. Help me, dear God."

As soon as I prayed those words, a challenge entered my mind. *Can you give up everything to follow Me?*

My breath caught in my throat. He was asking too much. I had spent three years building a world of protection around myself. Could I really let Him strip that away? It was a terrible choice, a choice I knew I wasn't ready to make just yet. I stumbled to my feet and struggled to ignore God's gentle tapping upon the door of my heart. I simply couldn't face Him yet in light of what He was asking of me.

not too many days later, I sat at home in my bedroom, tinkering with my keyboard, and suddenly my mind was filled with an expression of God's heart for me. It was a soft and gentle message, and even though I wasn't ready to accept it yet, I wrote the words down.

> Be still, My child, be still
> And know that I am here
> Be still, My child, be still
> Lay down all your fear.
>
> I know where you've been
> I've seen your pain
> My love for you
> Is always the same
> I'm still here whenever you call
> Be still and know that I am God.

Later I put music to the words and sang them to myself whenever I started to long for something beyond my empty world. God was calling me back to a quiet, still place at His feet. A place where my life focused on Him once again, rather than myself. I almost gave in to the calling. But the gradual softening of my heart abruptly ended when the first day of school showed itself all too soon . . .

"Hey are you coming to TJ's tonight? His parents are gone—major party-time!" A breathless Kelly called out to me as she dashed by my locker. Before I could reply, Lauren and Meagan had appeared out of nowhere enveloping me with non-stop excited chatter.

"You would not *believe* who I'm going out with now, Leslie! He is a *total* babe!" sing-songed Lauren as Meagan grabbed a tube of my lipstick from the top shelf of my locker and touched up her smile. "Hey, did you try out for cheerleading this year?" she wanted to know.

By the end of the day the peaceful moments of summer had faded into the background of my life and I was once again consumed by the social world I'd known for the past three years. Dating relationships once again came and went, stealing a piece of my heart each time.

Before I knew it, the months had flown by and it was nearly Christmas. I rarely had time to reflect on the fact that God had been working in my life just a short while ago. Already my Bible was buried, forgotten once again in my closet underneath my yearbook and homecoming dress. Whenever I was in my room and thoughts of my lackluster relationship with God would enter my mind, I would quickly flip on the radio or grab the phone and call a friend. As long as there was constant noise, I couldn't hear the still small knocking, causing my heart to ache with remorse. The kind of commitment God was calling me to was something that just didn't mix with my world.

But deep down I knew God wanted more of me. And somehow I also knew that soon it would come down to a decision—a decision between a shallow life of "playing church" while really living for myself, or total abandonment to my Lord Jesus Christ. I wasn't ready to face this dilemma, so I busied myself with more activities, more friendships, more dating, more youth group parties. I listened intently every time Kevin Richards shared his wisdom in the form of eloquent "devo" sessions. His version of Christianity suited my life quite well. Each time I heard his watered-down version of following Christ, it seemed to somehow buy me a little more time to live as I wanted—before the day I knew was coming soon—the day I would be required to make a choice.

Marky's Bedroom
1991

-eric-

i 'm sleepin' in here!" I boomed with my bassiest older brother voice. Following that announcement I tossed a folded-up blanket and sheet on the cot that had been set up next to my brother's bed. Without another word I strutted out of the room.

Over fourteen months had passed since I'd given up everything to Jesus Christ. And in that time I had gained a crystal clear vision for my life—I wanted to be molded into the likeness of Jesus Himself. I wanted everyone to see the loving God of the Universe when they interacted with my life. I desired my existence to be a little taste of heaven, whetting appetites for more of God.

I had given up everything I knew to give. Relationships with the opposite sex, my future as a medical doctor—I had even given up watching the Denver Broncos. I was certain there couldn't possibly be anything else that needed refining in my life.

I was home from college while waiting a few weeks to attend a missionary school. My college pre-med advisor had passionately warned me *not* to leave school during second semester due to the ill effects that decision would have on my attempt at a double major in biology and chemistry.

"You can be a doctor, Eric. Leaving now could seriously harm the continuity of your education." With knitted eyebrows he warned me, and with an irritated sigh he had withheld his blessing, deeming my spiritual adventure as "presumptuous and headstrong."

But days later, on my way home for Christmas break, a car crash clearly highlighted how fragile life really was and how important that

I entrusted even my future to God.

"I'm going to the missionary school!" I told my mom. "I'm not going to live this life cautiously, I'm going to live it with abandon!"

After all, I should have been dead. The policemen on the scene had told me.

"Rolling down that type of an incline—without a seat belt—and going sixty. . . . Boy, you shouldn't even be alive right now!"

Those type of words and that type of harrowing experience have a way of adding steel to your resolve. The truck my roommate and I were driving was totaled, but we both came out without a scratch and a whole lot for which to be thankful.

"I'm going!" I told my friends at college. "If things have ever been clear in my life, it's now! I want to go all out for God!"

Over fourteen amazing months I had transformed into something none of my old friends or acquaintances recognized. I was "weird," a "kook," and various other unmentionable names. I wasn't ashamed about what I believed anymore, because now I understood why I believed it—it was *real* to me!

But here I was under my parents' roof once again and the "new Eric" just disappeared. All I had to do was come within fifty feet of my mom, my dad, Krissy, or Marky and the "old Eric" re-emerged to wreak havoc on the Ludy world. I hated the "old" haughty, disrespectful, and critical Eric, but I was so conditioned to be "him" around my family that I guess I never thought anything of it. That is, until one unforgettable night when my grandparents' unexpected visit forced me out of my beloved bed and on to a cot next to my brother's. . . .

ow long are you gonna keep the light glaring in my face?" I bellowed with a raspy older brother toughness.

"I'm trying to read!" Marky passionately defended.

"Well, hurry up! There is a reason why people sleep at night—it's supposed to be dark!"

We both grunted our disapproval of the other's insensitivity and shifted in our nighttime habitats. As I lay on the stone-like cot my mind drifted to more pleasant things. I pondered Jesus. I thought about His goodness, His grace, His love. And so, while lying on my back, staring up at the light fixture on the ceiling, I inwardly prayed.

Jesus, make me like You! Whatever it takes, make me like You!

I sincerely meant that prayer. But after God immediately responded, I wished I'd never prayed it.

No way, God!

I squirmed, my heart pounding against my rib cage attempting to escape before it was too late.

I'll do anything . . . I just can't do . . . that!

With Marky reading his book next to me, I tossed, turned, and sweated trying to rationalize away what I knew God was nudging me to do.

God please! I know what I just prayed, and I really am willing to do anything. I just can't do . . . that!

It was probably the longest three and a half minutes of my life. As I lay there like a zombie staring at the light on the ceiling, I knew I had to make a choice.

I could run out of the room and deliberately ignore what God was asking of me. Or I could stay and (gulp) . . . ask forgiveness from my brother. And not just for my rudeness a few minutes back, but for my entire lifetime of older brother behavior.

The only thing that held me back was my raw pride. He was my stinkin' little brother, and I had never in my life intentionally shown weakness in front of him. Admitting I was wrong was the single most unpleasant form of showing weakness. I just couldn't!

God, I want to obey! I inwardly moaned.

I felt like I was going to burst with emotion. A deep sense of regret coursed through my heart and I saw clearly—as if my life were playing before my eyes on fast forward—all the times I had bruised Marky instead of blessed, all the times I had been critical rather than complimentary, and all the times I had held him at arm's length instead of reaching out to him as a brother.

"Mar—ky!" I finally spoke, my voice cracking.

"Yeah?" He spoke hesitantly in return, clearly remembering our most recent conversation.

"Uh, . . ." I searched for the words. "I'm sorry I railed on you about the light!"

"That's all right." He mumbled. "I'll turn it off in just a second."

He polished off the paragraph he was reading and then reached over to click off the light.

"Uh wait!" I said. "Hold on a minute!"

Marky looked over his shoulder at me, trying to figure out why I was acting so weird all of a sudden.

"Do you want me to turn off the light or not?" he groaned with a hint of sarcasm in his tone.

"Not yet." I stuttered. "I have something . . . that . . . I need to tell you."

Marky repositioned himself on his bed and turned to face my cot. He braced himself for the battle that was certain to come as a result of a talk with big brother Eric.

"Okay, I'm ready!" he announced, a little impatient to get it over with.

"Uh, . . ." I floundered. "Marky? I need to admit to you that I've been a horrible older brother!" I tried to chuckle to hold back the emotion surging within my chest.

Marky squirmed in his bed, repositioning his pillow to somehow avoid eye contact with me.

"I mean, I've never once complimented you . . . *ever!*"

Marky grunted his agreement.

"I have built such a barrier of pride between us that I can't let you into my life."

Then with a bubble of emotion rising in my throat I announced, "But I want to!"

Marky was dumbfounded. The conversation paused as my little brother took in the words he had always longed to hear. As he silently sat on his bed, long stored-up tears made their way to his eyes and then gently trickled down his cheeks.

I continued on, stumbling over my words, fighting off tears of my own. "Uh, I really want to be your friend."

Our ever-tough eyes were moist now and my face was struggling to keep it's composure. Marky hadn't seen me cry probably since I nearly electrocuted myself at age four. Even at the risk of looking like a blubbering idiot, I knew I had one more thing I had to say.

"Marky?"

And as I spoke his name, I lost my last remnant of older brother mystique. I began to cry. But it seemed God was beside me, cheering me on, wanting me to finish. I spoke through my choking tears.

"I don't know exactly how to say this so that you understand how deeply I mean it, but . . . uh, . . . could you . . . I mean . . . would you . . . please . . . forgive me?"

—eric—

eric?" Marky's voice interrupted the contemplative stillness. "Are you really convinced God is interested in our love lives?"

Staring out the dingy window at pigeons pecking for their daily sustenance I mumbled, "He'd better be!" and continued my careful study of my funny feathered friends.

"Well, I sure did mess up that part of my life!" Marky groaned and lifted his head from the pillow to assure himself I was listening.

"Yeah, so have I!" I responded.

"I can't believe how ridiculous it all seems now!" Marky took a swig from his water bottle and then plopped his head back down. "My life was consumed with girls. That's all I thought about. Dear God, did I mess things up!"

I turned around and began to stroll around the little fly-infested room. As if thinking out loud I announced, "When I get back home, I'm gonna have to call up every one of my old girlfriends and ask their forgiveness."

"That's a scary thought!" Marky bemoaned.

"Tell me about it!" I muttered under my breath.

"Well, I guess I could always tell all my old girlfriends," Marky interjected with energy, "that it was *your* fault I was such a jerk!"

I looked at Marky with a scowl that translated into "What are you talkin' about?"

"Well, you know darn good and well that you're the one who taught me how to sing love songs to the girls!"

We both laughed awkwardly at the embarrassing memory.

ittle did I ever dream I would be in Bulgaria as a missionary. But in Bulgaria, alongside my little brother *Marky*, this was way beyond the realm of possibility. Yet it was really happening—I was living out the impossible.

Something special happened between us when I had come home from college. We had begun to talk as friends, laugh at each other's jokes, even pray together. When he told me he was coming to Twin Oaks Ranch with me to go through missionary training, I could hardly believe my ears. But to Marky's profound amazement, I was thrilled!

There were times when my tough older brother side slunk out for the sneak attack, but with Marky's helpful reminders of our night of forgiveness, we somehow held onto our newfound friendship. And as proof of our deepening relationship, I confided in him about my convictions about God and my love life.

---

don't even know her yet," I shared with Marky as a Bulgarian fly buzzed around my head, "but if she could see me right now, I'd want her to know that I love her!"

I lifted up a piece of paper I'd been scribbling on, "I just wrote her a love letter, letting her know that I'm waiting for her."

"Well, let's see what ya' wrote!" Marky yelped excitedly.

"I'm not going to show *you!*" I barked incredulously. "I wrote it for her, *not* for my little brother!"

"Come on!" he jeered. "Just read me a line."

"Love, Eric." I poked. "You satisfied?"

Marky rolled his bright blue eyes and plopped his head back on his orange pillowcase.

eric

"You know, Eric?" Marky's eyes glazed over, revealing he was unwrapping a new idea. "Won't it be weird when we get married? I mean, life will completely change!"

We both pondered the wonder of wedded bliss for a few moments and then Marky added, "I guess you're gonna have to stop doing that disgusting throat clearing thing in the morning!"

"Well, *you're* gonna have to stop snoring!" I jabbed back.

"My wife will be soothed by my snore!" Marky defended.

"Yeah right! And *my* wife will be soothed by my disgusting throat clearing thing!"

Marky rolled his eyes and once again reached for his trusty water bottle.

I threw myself on my bed and joined Marky in staring at the ceiling. (I guess that was our position for deep meaningful discussion.)

"I've always looked for a girl who would turn my *head,*" Marky mumbled, eyes transfixed on yet another Bulgarian fly walking on the ceiling. "But, for the first time in my life, I realize that what I really want, above anything else, is a woman that turns my *heart.*"

"I like that." I admitted reflectively. "I guess I'm after the same thing. I want a woman who loves Jesus even more than she loves me."

"I want a woman that is willing to go anywhere and do anything for God!" Marky added with newfound conviction. "I never thought I'd say this but . . . maybe someone like Krissy!"

A reminiscent smile creased my face as I pondered Krissy. For years Marky and I had mocked and ridiculed her. And here we were, both agreeing that we wanted to spend the rest of our lives with someone *like* her.

"Yeah. Someone like Krissy." As I spoke those words, I realized what a treasure she had stored up for *her* future husband. She was twenty-three years old and had set her life aside for God and purity for her future husband, since she was twelve. "Some guy is going to be *real* lucky to get her!"

"He'd better appreciate it!" Marky added while tensing his jaw muscles and letting out a protective grunt.

We lay there for a good ten minutes just thinking. Bulgarian flies buzzed, pigeons cooed, and the sun disappeared behind the horizon. Marky and I had become a team. We were finally discovering what brotherhood was all about.

Marky finally broke the silence.

"Are you really serious, Eric, about not dating another girl until 'she' comes into your life?"

"Yeah!" I said after a few seconds of evaluation. "I don't quite know how it's all going to work yet, but yeah, I am!"

"What if it's forty more years?"

I let out a laugh at the horrifying thought.

"If it's forty more years till I meet my wife . . ." I paused and wrinkled my eyebrows together with resolution, "then she'd better be worth the wait!"

Eric's Love Letter
August 15th, 1991

—eric—

my Girl,

I'm sitting in a quaint little room overlooking the enchanting city of Sofia. I wish you were here. The view is spectacular; but more than anything I wish we could share this moment together. I'm realizing that every moment we spend apart adds even greater beauty to the time in the future when we will spend our lives together as one.

I want you to know that I'm waiting for you. I try and pray for you every night. I ask God to protect you, mold you, and prepare you as my wife. I know He's crafting me into a godly man who fears the Lord and who will be sensitive to His Spirit. He's breaking me now, I'm certain, so that He can build me up strong as a leader and as a true gentle man.

I love you even now. Even before I meet you. Even before I lay eyes on you. And no matter how long it takes I will be here, faithfully waiting for you to discover that love that is yours already. My heart longs for the day I can read this, and the many other letters I have written, to you.

He is perfectly faithful!

Love,
Your boy, Eric

The Toyota Camry
1991

eric, what's wrong?" My mom delicately inquired, her eyes carefully studying the upcoming traffic jam on 6th Avenue.

"Uh, . . . I don't know!" I despondently moaned.

"Are you throwing yourself a pity party?" Her eyes took a quick peek at me slouched in the passenger's seat and a smirk danced across her face.

My mom could smell a pity party a mile away. "Yeah," I groaned while my eyes studied the crack in the dashboard and my right hand fidgeted with the city map I was utilizing to navigate. "I've never been so lonely!"

"Do you really miss your college friends?" she questioned with a healthy dose of compassion in her voice.

"Yeah! I just feel like my life is going nowhere." I shifted in my seat, set down the map and continued. "When I was at college I knew who I was and I knew where I was going. Life was easy!"

I paused as my mom carefully ventured around a stalled car in the right lane. We both gawked at the forlorn owner of the car as he pleaded his case with the police officer.

"I don't feel like I fit in anymore." I continued. "I used to be liked by everybody. Now I just feel like everyone thinks I'm this nutcase who needs a stay in a mental ward."

"Oh, Eric! I don't think anyone thinks that!" my mom comforted.

"Yeah they do!" I remonstrated. "Becoming a doctor was honorable and respectable. Being a missionary is just above cleaning toilets at Los Burrittos! When I had a girlfriend I looked masculine and complete. Now I have people wondering if I'm gay or if I'm scared of girls!"

My mom silently waited for me to continue, knowing I was in desperate need of a good emotional dumping.

"I sometimes feel like going out and getting a girl just to prove to everyone I'm a man!" I grunted and picked up the map again, only to throw it into the backseat. I was agitated, hurt, and depressed all at the same time.

"Now what am I doing?" I begged for understanding. "I'm studying how to be a singer. What am I thinking?"

"You mean," my mother was quick to point out, "what is everyone else thinking?"

Again she hit the nail right on the head. I knew I was right where God wanted me. I was home restoring relationships with my family, (even this simple talk with my mom was unusual and a big step in the right direction) and I was gaining a skill that, for years, I'd had a passion to learn. I wanted to learn to sing in a way that could impart truth into people's lives, encourage them, even invite them into the throne room of God. But even though I knew I was right where God wanted me, all I could think about was what everyone else was thinking about my whacko life.

"Eric?" a maternal lecture was brewing, "Could I say a few things to you?"

Staring out the window I grunted my approval.

"You are an amazing young man!" Her words weren't corrective as I had been expecting. "And Eric, God has a plan for you that is beyond your wildest imagination! Right now, this season of loneliness is preparing you for leadership!"

As she spoke, a gentle peace and a wave of hope washed over me.

"When Jesus gets a hold of your life, one of the first things that happens is that your life no longer blends in with the rest of this world." She again took a peek over at me wondering if her words were falling on listening or deaf ears.

"Your values have changed, your motivations have changed, and Eric, even the way you speak has changed. You are a new person. You are exhibiting Jesus now!"

She paused and took in a breath.

"Always remember, Eric. Jesus didn't fit in!"

"But what am I accomplishing in life right now?" I begged.

"Eric, God doesn't care about you accomplishing things, He cares about you obeying. When you obey, it's truly amazing what you accomplish!"

Again we temporarily paused our conversation as she exited onto Wadsworth and chose to go through a yellow light instead of stopping.

"Just think what God is doing in your life!"

I turned my head to look at her, wondering what she meant by that.

"You have a brother who feels like the luckiest man in the world. He has his big brother kneeling with him every morning at the Ridgeview High flagpole to pray. He has you for a close friend for the first time in his life."

"You are making your mother's heart burst with pride, Honey! I feel like *I* finally have a relationship with you too. Eric, I have prayed your entire life that one day you would come to know Jesus like you do right now."

Then she looked over at me with a gleam in her eye and said,

"And Eric, you will be forever blessed by the decision you have made to be faithful to your future spouse."

She reached out and took my hand and concluded, "She is

going to have to be one very special young woman to put up with a radical like you!"

She did it! She made me smile. As much as I wanted to continue attending my very own private pity party, I just couldn't. My mom was right. I needed to start looking at life through God's eyes instead of my own. Because God was in complete control, and all this loneliness, all this pain, all this patience would one day pay off. One day it would all hopefully make sense.

Part Two:

the friendship

Creekside Community Church

—eric—

i s this where you guys decided to go to church?" Don inquired, his voice a soft whisper in my ear.

"At least it's closer than forty-five minutes away!" Marky jabbed back.

"I don't see any black dudes here! There's no rhythm here, man! I don't know if I can bear to see two more white brothers lose their rhythm." Don Randolph, the Ludy family's good "black dude" friend, knew how to laugh. It just seemed that all too often it was at *Ludy* expense.

"Well, if you started coming to Creekside with us," I added, "we would have at least *one* black dude!" We all chuckled a little too loud and heard "shhh's" coming from the row behind us.

"We'll miss you both, man!" Don whispered to Marky and me in all seriousness as the lights dimmed and the music started. The Christmas play had officially begun. Little kids stormed across the stage squawking out their lines and joyfully howling out familiar Christmas tunes.

Since arriving back from missionary school, Marky and I had searched high and low for a church home. We tried out various denominations, quite a few different cultural expressions, and most recently had become good friends with Don Randolph while attending his "church with rhythm" on the other end of town.

Yet after all was said and done, we decided that we needed to be at Creekside Community where my parents were. At first attending a church different than my parents' made us feel more grown-up, but in the end we decided that family was what church was all about.

"That kid in the blue is pretty darn good!" Marky softly muttered, gaining agreeable nods from Don and me.

"How 'bout the kid with the hair sticking up?" I carefully whispered.

The kid with the hair sticking up was studiously removing various treasures from his belly button as the rest of the children's choir danced across the stage. To our amusement his mother was backstage, red as Superman's cape, trying to get him to focus on his dance steps rather than his newfound supply of lint.

There was laughter and cheering, sighing and booing. The crowd was really involved. I think Don, Marky, and I were leading the rabble. There were chuckles and snorts. There was rooting and applause—and amidst it all there appeared on stage . . . a princess.

Creekside Community Church
December 15, 1991

-leslie-

g reat job up there, Les!" beamed Rachel Anderson, a lovely
older woman who seemed to have taken a liking to me ever
since my family had begun attending this church last year. Creekside
was a small family of believers which didn't even have a youth group.
But I didn't mind. Kevin Richards' high-energy meetings had started
getting old after three years.

"Thank you," I answered, returning her smile. The small church
sanctuary was simmering with laughter and pleasant conversation as
the cast of Christmas-play performers, mostly elementary school kids
and a few good-sported adults, merged with the audience of friends
and family members.

I scanned the crowded room for my parents. I was relieved the
Christmas play was finally over. I had reluctantly agreed to participate as one of the main characters in the cast, mostly because my
parents had strongly "encouraged" me to. It had actually turned out
to be a fun experience, though I wouldn't have admitted it to them.
Now that it was over, my mind was on my sixteenth birthday—
which was the following day. My parents had planned a birthday
dinner at a fancy Italian restaurant for later that night, and my
stomach was starting to growl impatiently at the thought of the
pasta primavera I was going to order.

I felt a little rush of excitement every time I thought about the
fact that I was almost sixteen. For some reason, I had always imagined
that something "special" would happen to me in my sixteenth year.
After all, my sixteenth birthday fell on the sixteenth of December.

"Sweet sixteen, Leslie!" my friends had joked. "It *has* to be your lucky year!"

Maybe now that I'm sixteen my love life will change, was the fleeting thought that ran through my mind as I continued searching for my parents. *Maybe I'll find out that Prince Charming really does exist after all, and my childhood fairy tale wishes will finally come true!* I stopped myself short. I rarely allowed unrealistic thoughts to enter my mind. Now a sarcastic voice inside quickly squelched that line of dreaming. *Get real. Don't dream about something that doesn't exist. It's too late for someone like you to find true love anyway. You've completely ruined that area of your life.*

I could find no trace of my parents, so I turned to exit the sanctuary and look elsewhere, still shaking my head to somehow erase my foolish torrent of thoughts. *The man of your dreams doesn't exist, Leslie, and even if he did, he would never want you now.* With that stubborn conclusion, I closed the subject and leaned against the heavy door leading to the lobby. As the door swung open, I suddenly found myself staring into the richest pair of brown eyes I'd ever seen.

"Hi!" the young man spoke with an enthusiastic smile. He was tall and broad-shouldered, and looked about twenty-one or twenty-two years old. His curly jet-black hair complemented his olive skin tone. As he smiled, his dark eyes sparkled and a small mole above the left side of his mouth added to his look of boyish enthusiasm.

He seemed to be waiting for a reply, so I quickly found my voice. "Um, hi," I answered hesitantly.

"Are you Leslie?" he hurriedly asked. When I nodded, he launched into an animated explanation. "My name's Eric Ludy. I just talked to your mom. She said you are a voice student and that you write songs. I'm just starting to get into that field, so I wondered if I could talk to you about it sometime. Hey, great job up there tonight by the way."

At his easy manner, I relaxed and smiled back at him as we chatted about music and song writing. For years, every young man I had interacted with had been expecting some sort of flirtatious game. I had learned how to play the game and put on the act—but I had almost forgotten how to have a normal, healthy, friendly conversation with someone of the opposite sex. Yet in those brief moments of dialogue, I felt like a real person again—instead of being seen as a sex object.

I felt strangely refreshed around this man named Eric Ludy—so much older than me, yet so considerate and polite. I was intrigued by his constant smile and energetic attitude toward life. I could tell instantly that he was unlike any young man I'd ever known.

"You ready to go Les?" my dad's voice suddenly called from across the lobby. I waved at him and then turned back to my new-found friend.

"It was nice meeting you, Eric. I'd be happy to tell you anything I know about recording studios. Are you going to be here Sunday?"

"Yeah, I've just started attending church here with my parents," he answered back with a grin. "See you Sunday."

A warm feeling flooded me as I jogged out to the parking lot to meet my family. I had no thought of a relationship with Eric Ludy— he hadn't done anything to indicate an attraction or interest. In fact, he didn't even strike me as the type of guy who was constantly on the prowl for shallow dating relationships. I knew he was different and hoped I would get to know him better. Eric Ludy seemed like the type of person that could be a lifelong friend.

Later that night I sat in Fratelli's Italian Restaurant gazing at a beautiful topaz and diamond ring my parents had presented to me for my sixteenth birthday.

"It's gorgeous!" I breathed in delight as I slipped it on. I hugged them both tightly and whispered, "Thank you so much. I love you both."

I thought I saw tears glisten in my mother's eyes. In that brief moment, I felt like an innocent little girl again, and the pain of the past few years seemed to lose some of its bite.

I knew my life was still not where it should be. More than once over the school year, I had wished that I could rewind my life to that night at Evergreen Christian Camp when everything was so clear—before I had been hopelessly entangled once more in the intricate web of popularity.

But tonight, I felt a glimpse of what my life *could* be, should I ever find the strength to focus on what truly mattered. The beautiful jeweled ring I'd been given seemed to be a symbol of hope on the horizon, like the promise of spring rains after a long harsh winter. I longed for my life to change this year—my sweet sixteenth year. Somehow I felt that change coming. But it wouldn't be until a few months later that I would realize how drastically this change would take its shape.

1422 South Newport Way

—eric—

n o way!" I moaned in disbelief while my hand reached for my half-full mug of piping spiced cider resting on the edge of the baby grand piano. "There is absolutely no way you wrote that song when you were fourteen!"

The cute young girl at the piano didn't look up, she just stared at the piano keys and gave an embarrassed little shrug of her shoulders.

"Do you have any more?" my mom chimed in from her strategically stationed "stereo-sound" Lazy-Boy recliner.

"Uh, . . ." the young girl with emerald eyes stuttered. But before she could answer, Marky created a stir in the living room, hopping around moaning "Ohhh, hot, hot, hot, hot!" and blowing on his mug of cider. Then when he realized he had seriously impaired our flow of conversation he looked up sheepishly and muttered, "Sorry!"

All eyes again returned to the little musician seated at the piano.

"Play us another one!" my dad encouraged.

"Yeah, keep it going!" Marky added despite his scalded tongue.

"Uh, . . ." she hesitated, "I'd like to hear Eric sing one of his."

All eyes turned to me. Marky didn't waste any time adding his two cents: "We don't want to hear him. We hear him all the time. Come on, Leslie, play us one more!"

But the brilliant little musician had made up her mind. Defying the "man of scalded tongue" she arose from her seat and beckoned me to sit and play.

eric

Such a young girl. Yet she intrigued me. I was used to talking with the likes of Eleanor Radcliff, Jenny Williams, Brenda Dykstra, Trina Simms, and Keri Wooden up at college. Intellectual, confident, and sassy. Nineties women who were quick to cut me down and slow to build me back up. This little girl was different. She was intellectual but not ostentatious, she was confident but sweetly humble, and she was not sassy but more mysterious and dignified. I found myself fascinated by this young woman. She seemed rather a paradox—beautiful and bold yet humble and sweet, trapped within a world of popularity yet seeking somehow, some way to let it all go and give Jesus Christ her all.

From the moment I first laid eyes on her, she had a song in her heart. I could see her passionate soul longing for a deeper intimacy with Jesus. I knew right away that this young girl was different, she was special, and God had a protective and jealous guardianship over her heart and life. I wanted to be an encouragement to her. I could give her a glimpse into a deeper life, a liberated life, a surrendered life. What I didn't know was how much she would teach me.

That was amazing, Eric!" she whispered after I finished my song on the piano. "I don't know if I've ever heard anyone play and sing with so much passion and conviction." She paused and let her words sink in, then she spoke to me in a way that makes a boy a man, and a man a warrior. She simply said, "The world needs to hear you sing!"

She knew how to reach me. She was different and that fascinated me— I only wished she wasn't so young. There was a clearly established boundary in my life. I guess you could call it the "Brad Binks' baby sister" boundary. I mean, this young girl had been in junior high when I first went off to college! I could be a friend, I could be a brother, I could be an example of a man of God, but under no circumstances could I ever be more than that. I was twenty-one, she was sixteen—enough said.

311 Rambling Rose Road
February 2, 1992

-eric-

"Welcome to our home!" Janet Runkles warmly sang to the herd of Ludys standing on her front doorstep in the cold.

The Ludys shuffled into the toasty entryway and allowed the newfound warmth to thaw our toes and the scent of freshly baked lasagna to thaw out our digestive enzymes.

"Hey!" was the predictable shout out of both Marky's and my larynx as Leslie and the rest of her family—Rich, her dad, and younger brothers David and John—emerged into the coat-swapping, boot-removing, nose-wiping hallway. Excited hugs were passed around and introductions were made to Cheyenne, the Runkles' personable golden retriever.

"What a beautiful home!" my mom was quick to point out.

The rest of us Ludys joined in on the "oohs" and "ahhs" as we looked around at Janet's amazing ability to make a house into a home.

"So that's the piano," my dad excitedly rang, "where all that great music is written?"

Again we all added our "oohs" and "ahhs" and Leslie added her cute little shoulder shrug to signify that she was a little embarrassed by the glowing compliment.

The lasagna was devoured with minimal damage to Janet's carpeting and upholstery. The conversation was animated—full of missionary adventures, tales of Ludy childhoods, and bizarre happenings with a Ludy-ish sort of spin.

My smile was as big as usual throughout the night. But deep inside I was struggling.

two years ago on this very day, February 2nd, God had changed my life. I'd finished the book my sister had given me, I had opened my life to God, and He had begun to change me. Every year now something special had happened on this, my spiritual anniversary. But tonight I felt forgotten. God had overlooked his little boy, Eric, and had somehow forgotten to check His Daytimer.

The dinner table conversation continued. I laughed when I needed to laugh, I shook my head in understanding when necessary, and even complimented the chef on a lasagna well done. But I was crying inside. I had approached this day with an expectancy and tremendous hope. I just knew God had something special in store. But here I was at a family's house—a family I barely knew—feeling like midnight was just a few short hours away, and my special day with God would be over.

"Would you all mind," Rich Runkles spoke up, "if we moved into the living room and got a little more comfortable?"

We all stood up and moseyed on into the other room. David and John were given the duty of bringing in kitchen chairs to provide a seat for the many extra bottoms present. My mom thanked Janet for the recipe card that read "Lone Star Lasagna." Marky had Cheyenne roll over and rubbed her furry tummy. My dad and Rich bantered about the injustice of litigation lawyers. Leslie asked if any of us wanted more tea or coffee. And I just sat on the Runkles' couch, paralyzed with sorrow.

When everyone finally settled in to their seats, all mugs were filled, and Leslie sat down, Rich asked a question:

"I was wondering if we could spend some time praying?"

Of course all of us were eager and excited.

"Sure!" my dad exclaimed on behalf of all Ludys present.

We closed our eyes and a tremendous stillness filled the room. Everything was silent for about three minutes before Janet started the audible portion of our prayer time.

"Lord," she prayed, "thank you for this special night spent with this special family!"

The words continued but my mind couldn't stay focused. *God, I pleaded internally, please let me know You are there and that You care.*

As the minutes passed, prayers were prayed by everyone around the room. The only one who didn't contribute was me. I felt like I needed to prove to the Runkles family that I was a "prayer warrior," but I just had nothing in my heart and mind to pray.

Amidst one of the silent pockets of time during the prayer, I opened my eyes and looked up. Everyone's eyes were tightly shut. Cheyenne, the dog, was vying for attention from David's right hand, Marky was scratching his nose, my mom was quietly whispering to God, and right across from me a beautiful young lady was seated, hands reverently cupped around her face. When my eyes caught sight of her praying, it was as if a voice like an August wind brushed through my heart and spoke to my mind, "Eric, this is *her.*"

I was very cognizant of the fact that there was an enemy of my soul. And if I had ever been convinced he was active and at work trying to destroy my life it was right then. Right in the middle of a prayer time, Satan had the gall to try and poison my motives and thoughts towards this little sixteen-year-old girl. I was convinced God had put her into my life so that I could encourage her with an example of a godly man. I was certain it was my duty before God to protect her as a brother and to be a trustworthy friend. Granted, I was fascinated by her and I thought she was quite beautiful. But before God and a room full of witnesses I would have testified to the fact that never could it be right and honorable for a twenty-one-year-old to think such presumptuous thoughts about a sixteen-year-old. I knew God wasn't speaking. I knew the enemy was.

As the prayer time came to a close, I felt very unspiritual. For some reason God had forgotten me on our anniversary. I wouldn't have admitted it then, but I was angry with God for disregarding me, angry at myself for not proving to the Runkles' family how well I could pray, and angry at the enemy for attempting to poison my thoughts toward my little sister Leslie.

In this overwrought emotional state I attempted to slip my arms into my coat sleeves and tie the shoestrings on my boots. All the appropriate "goodbyes" and "let's do it again soons" were exchanged and we Ludys turned to leave when Janet interjected my name.

"Eric?" she cautiously spoke.

"Yes?" I pleasantly replied while yanking my hands into my black leather gloves.

"Uh," she hesitated.

The smile on my face masked the emotion within my heart.

"Uh," she continued while biting her lip and lowering her gaze to the ground. "I feel that I need to tell you something."

I felt like this woman, whom I barely knew, was peering into my soul. It was as if she was reading me like a newspaper article and preparing her critique.

"Go for it!" I awkwardly answered.

"Well," she carefully sighed, "I think that God wants you to know that what was spoken to you tonight was from Him."

My mind eagerly searched for an experience that night that could possibly have been termed "a message from God." But no matter how much I wanted Janet to be right, I was certain that God hadn't spoken anything to me that night. In fact, the truth be known, He'd forgotten about me.

"Does that make any sense?" she sweetly questioned.

"Uh, . . ." I stuttered. "Uh, . . . I'll pray about it." How could I tell her that she couldn't be farther from the truth?

As I strolled out into the cold night air I felt lonely and forgotten. *Where are you God? Where is our celebration?* Lying in bed that chilly February eve, I prayed that God would one day make sense of that night. With a pang in my heart I drifted off to sleep, totally unaware of the glimmer in God's eye and the exuberant smile on His loving face.

Romero's Pizzeria
Tyler, Texas, 1992

-leslie-

hey Les, are you getting your gastric juices pumpin'?" Eric asked mischievously while his brother Mark made a hilarious grimace over Eric's shoulder. I shot an amused glance at David, my twelve-year-old brother seated next to me on the bright red plastic bench. Before I could think of a joking comment to throw into the mixture of meaningless conversation, a waiter placed a sizzling tray of hot pizza on our table amidst loud cheers and exclamations from the Ludy boys.

As we all bowed our heads, I noticed the enthusiasm with which Eric prayed, even if just for a meal. His passionate love for the Lord was contagious. Ever since my mom had spontaneously suggested that David and I join Mark and him on this road trip to Texas to visit their old missionary school, life had been full of adventure.

Had it really only been four days ago that I was sitting in algebra reading a note from Amanda about her new boyfriend? My life back home seemed worlds away now. It was February, the middle of my sophomore year—but for some reason my parents had felt comfortable allowing me to take a week off from school. Almost equally as amazing was the fact that I actually felt eager to get away from my all-consuming social life for a while. Normally I would have been in a state of panic, wondering if my friends would forget about me or if the new guy I had my eye on would decide to date someone else while I was away.

But as the Ludy's red Toyota Camry sped south on I-25, each mile seemed to separate me from that world—not just physically, but emotionally as well. The 17-hour drive to the missionary school had been anything but boring. Eric and Mark were full of life, constantly making up creative games or songs or jokes to keep us laughing the entire trip. We'd had serious talks as well. Eric and Mark had shared the amazing spiritual journey God had taken them both on just a couple of years earlier. As I observed their lives and listened to their stories, I found my heart pierced with a deep and inexplicable conviction. Here were two young men who had purpose and meaning so far beyond anything I ever experienced in my shallow world of popularity, or even what I had observed in Christian circles. My soul had been especially gripped when Eric had shared about his decision to "abandon himself" completely to Jesus Christ. It had been a radical choice he made . . .

"I was in pre-med, and doing what I had always dreamed of," he shared animatedly, "but I realized that, even though I'd been a Christian since I was five, I had never asked God what *He* wanted to do with my life."

Eric had gone on to tell me how he made the decision to leave college and everything that made sense in his life, and become part of a missionary school along with his brother. He gave his future and dreams and hopes and plans to God. During the missionary school, he and Mark had both discovered a deep, intimate relationship with Christ that they'd never known before. And they had learned what "abandonment to Christ" was truly about. Now they lived on the cutting edge of faith, always expectant for God to work, always on the lookout for how God might want to use their lives in big ways or small, every moment of every day.

As I listened to Eric and Mark share their stories, an intense sense of longing crept over my entire being—longing for the kind of intimacy with my Savior that these men had found. Longing for a life that truly lived what it professed to believe. Longing for complete surrender to Jesus Christ.

⟵

ric and Mark Ludy's purposeful existence was only one of the tools God used in my life that week. From the moment I stepped out of the car onto the missionary base, I could feel a strong pull upon my heart from my Creator. For the first time in years, I was away from my social world—the phone was not ringing, the radio was not blaring, and my frenzied life was not beckoning. I had momentarily escaped the whirlwind that had cluttered my mind and thinking for years. And it seemed that God was giving me a perspective that I'd never had before.

All week long I met individuals who were passionate about their love for Jesus Christ. Not just in the words they spoke—in the way they lived. I was amazed by such *radical* Christianity—these people revolved their whole lives around their faith in God. They didn't just give Him time on Sundays or Wednesday nights, they brought Him into the center of everything they did.

For years I had been wrapped up in my own little world. It took a week of separation from that world—a week of being with complete strangers in a strange place—for God to get my attention.

Sitting in the cafeteria one afternoon, I picked at a plateful of soggy taco salad and listened to the banter of conversation between Eric, Mark, and an enthusiastic missionary couple, Brad and Katie.

"I spent the first thirty-five years of my adult life focused on making money and being successful," Brad said, his bright blue eyes full of intensity, "and then God got through to me. I realized I was calling myself a Christian but my priorities in life were money and accomplishments, not God. I said I was living for God, but I was really only living for myself. Every time I went to church on Sunday morning, I'd make up my mind to change my life and my priorities, but then Monday morning at work I'd be sucked right back into my old lifestyle."

"So what finally happened that you ended up here at Twin Oaks?" Mark inquired while ruthlessly spearing an olive with his fork.

"We took a weekend away to the ocean," Katie recalled, "and after spending time away from all the busyness we'd lived in for so long, we both realized how empty our life was. We sort-of looked at each other and decided that we didn't want the next thirty-five years of our lives to be like the first thirty-five."

"I had felt for a long time that God wanted me to go onto the mission field," Brad added, drizzling enchilada sauce onto his refried beans. "And I just kept ignoring that little voice inside, speaking to my heart. But that night I knew it was time to do something radical. We knelt down by the couch and gave God control of every area of our lives."

"And life has never been the same since!" Katie finished happily.

I looked down at the tangled mess of lettuce and taco chips on my plate. *How can people make such extreme decisions with their lives? How can they be so happy after giving up money and security?* I wondered to myself. A few weeks ago, I realized, I would have thought this kind of radical Christianity was ridiculous. But now, my heart was strangely stirred by their passion, their enthusiasm, their radiance.

Later that evening, I took a walk beside a field of glorious wild flowers. As the crisp air stung my cheeks, I found a seat on a chilly tree stump and listened to the buzzing and singing of junebugs and crickets. Once again, I felt a tug on my heart, the same gentle pull I'd been experiencing since I'd arrived a few days earlier. Only now it was stronger, too intense to ignore. God was speaking to me. I pursed my lips together and tried to still the pounding of blood in my ears and quiet the butterflies in my stomach. After all the times I had ignored Him, after all the years of living for myself and allowing so much sin to creep into my life, what would God say to me? Would He strike me with some terrible punishment for turning away from Him? Would He proclaim horrible judgment over my life?

Come back to Me, precious child.

Such a soft, beckoning whisper. I began to weep quietly, wondering how God could still love me so much after I'd compromised in so many ways. I was never so aware of His tender, tear-filled eyes, longing for me to find refuge in His arms like a gentle shepherd. My heart broke. Slowly, I knelt down on the cold ground.

"Forgive me, Lord. I've been living for myself. Forgive me for trying to fit you into my life . . . now I want to build my whole life around You. Show me how to truly make You first in my life, Lord Jesus."

I was shaking when I got off my knees, and the inward trembling didn't stop for the next two days. In my heart of hearts, I knew there were radical steps ahead I must take in order to build my life completely around Him.

***

G od's really been working in your heart lately, hasn't He Leslie?" Jessie, a bright, friendly young missionary student had befriended me during my stay at Twin Oaks, and even in the short time I had known her, I knew she genuinely cared about my life. Now, as we walked side by side along the road leading to the worship center, she was reading into my soul. I smiled hesitantly, not sure how much to reveal to her. After all, she was practically a stranger. But as I glanced into her sparkling brown eyes, I was instantly disarmed.

"Uh, yeah, He really has been," I answered quietly. "It's kind of hard to explain. But I really feel I need to make some major changes in my life in order to make Him my number one focus. And . . . I'm, um, just kind of scared of what those changes might be."

Jessie nodded in understanding. "Let me just encourage you with something, Leslie," she said as she kicked a pebble with her right tennis shoe. "God never asks us to do something that He doesn't give us the strength to accomplish. And whatever He is asking of you, it's only because He wants the very best for you. You are His princess, and He is jealously guarding your life. It may seem like a sacrifice to obey Him, and you may not understand all the reasons why, but in the end, it will be the greatest blessing."

Twin Oaks Ranch
February 1992

—eric—

a pair of dirty socks flew through the air, landing harmlessly on a blue backpack stationed in the southeast corner of the quaint hotel room.

"What in the world are you doing?" I stammered with older brother toughness while perusing a brochure on supporting missions work in Azerbaijan.

"Your initials are on them. They're yours!" Marky grunted in reply while focused intently on packing up his dirty clothes for the return trip to Colorado.

"What do you mean they're mine?" I argued, while attempting to maintain my focus on my intriguing brochure. "You wore 'em, you pack 'em!"

Like every brotherly quarrel, we howled for a couple minutes about nothing, ranted about responsibility and fairness, raved about serious violations of property rights, then finally compromised and each packed one of the brownish socks in our backpack.

After we both stacked our belongings next to the hotel room door I looked at my watch, rolled my eyes and moaned, "We've still got fifteen minutes."

We had some time to blow prior to heading off for our final meal at Twin Oaks ranch before returning home. I flopped on the bed and let out a monster groan. Marky picked up the brochure on Azerbaijan and quickly leafed through it. Silence filled the room for a couple minutes, me staring at the fly meandering across the ceiling, and Marky searching the "welcome" basket for other forms of literature.

Marky broke the silence.

"What do ya think of Leslie?"

I continued to stare at the Texas fly but responded, "I think she's . . . um . . . nice."

Marky chuckled and stared at me with an enormous smile on his face.

After about fifteen seconds I met his smirky face with a glare of disdain and squawked, "What?"

His smirky smile remained and he graciously offered a few more irritating chuckles.

"What's your problem?" I yelped. "What do you find so amusing?"

Marky, in perfect little brother form, with a giggle in his throat mused, "I think ya like her!"

With that I hopped up from the squeaky bed and defended my name and honor. "She is a little girl, you idiot! If anybody likes her, it would be *you!*"

Marky recognized that he had struck a sensitive chord and he continued to pluck at it. With his smirky look unaltered and his resolve unfazed he ventured onward into dangerous waters.

"Do ya think I'm stupid or something?" He spoke with passion. "I can tell when you like a girl. You are SO obvious!"

My pointer finger emerged from its holster and directed itself at Marky's obnoxious smirk.

"THAT is totally ridiculous!" I blared while veins in my neck protruded and my face turned a fiery red. "You're the one always trying to sit next to her at meals and singing lines of love songs to grab her attention. I know what you're doing! YOU like her!"

"Ohhh!" Marky got excited. "What about you telling her you can tutor her on her algebra? Huh? What was that but a romantic proposition?"

"Give me a break!" I bellowed. "She's just a little girl! FIVE years younger than me! I'm not a fool!"

We stared at each other for a few moments in silence then Marky added the clincher. "I think you're going to marry her!"

At twenty-one I was certain of two things: There was a God in the universe, and I was NOT going to marry Leslie Runkles. I mean wasn't it obvious to everyone? She was two-and-a-half years younger than my little baby brother. Things like that don't happen to "normal" people on the planet Earth. For two months, since I first watched her walk onto that stage singing, I had battled to keep my thoughts pure toward this amazing young lady. Observing her life and attitude on this trip to Twin Oaks had only furthered my fascination with her and only caused me to tighten the reins on my thought life to make sure I honored her and respected her in my mind at all times. Since I was absolutely certain there would never be a possibility of anything beyond friendship, it was my goal to think about her and treat her life delicately in light of that pressing reality.

Marky had crossed a sacred proprietary boundary. He had challenged the integrity of his big brother Eric. It was nothing but malarkey from Marky! My mind raced for a way to cut him down, crush his ego, strip away his smirky smile. "You are so clueless!" I floundered, not quite stripping him of his chuckle-filled face. Then in all seriousness, I forecast what I honestly believed to be the future reality of Marky Ludy:

"I think YOU are going to marry Leslie Runkles!"

If I were a prophet I would need to be stoned for my glaring inaccuracy. Marky, fortunately, did not end up marrying little Leslie Runkles, and still to this day I'm missing a match for a brownish sock stored away in the top drawer of my dresser.

The Toyota Camry

-leslie-

at exactly five o'clock A.M., David, Eric, Mark and I sleepily piled into the Ludy's red Toyota Camry to begin the long trek back to Colorado. Eric, I learned from some of his old dorm-mates, had been known in missionary school as the P.T.M. (Perfectly Timed Man). After this road trip together, I could easily understand why he earned such a nickname.

"Eric, why don't we just sleep in tomorrow and leave after breakfast?" Mark had complained loudly the night before as Eric carefully set the alarm on his watch for 4:30 A.M.

"Marky," Eric replied with grim determination, "that would get us to Colorado at three o'clock in the morning! Rich and Janet would never trust us again if we get their children home at three in the morning!"

Though I would have preferred to sleep in myself, I was impressed with Eric's debate skills. In the end, Eric won the argument and now here we were, cruising along the Texas interstate as the sun began spreading its first rays along the horizon.

As the hours passed, my mind raced along with the hundreds of yellow lines that flashed by in a blur.

"Hey, Les, why are you being so quiet?" David remarked from the front seat as he unsuccessfully attempted to refold a mangled road map.

Mark peered mischievously at me through the rear view mirror while Eric studied me with a furrowed brow from the next seat over. They had noticed my silence as well.

I cleared my throat. "Well, I'm just . . . thinking, I guess," I said in response to their merciless scrutiny.

If there was one thing I had learned about Ludys however, it was that they love to dig down inside a person's soul and talk about what's really going on. Eric had already repositioned himself for a "serious" talk by setting aside his well-worn copy of a C.S Lewis book, unwinding his seatbelt to face me, and knitting his eyebrows to signify an attitude of deep thought.

"So tell us what God did in your life this week," he asked, grinning with expectancy. Mark's eyes continued to dance eagerly in the rear view mirror as he set the Camry onto cruise control at sixty-seven miles per hour. David had settled back into his seat with an open bag of cheese popcorn, his ears perked with interest. I realized that this road crew was ready to hear me spill my guts. Well, why not? I reasoned. I *needed* to talk. I wanted to verbalize what was happening inside of me before I re-entered my old, familiar life back home.

"God's been really challenging me this week," I finally said after a long pause, "to build my life completely around Him. To change my priorities. To really make Him first, not just in the words I say, but in the way I live."

"So, what do you think that means on a practical level?" Mark chimed in as he reached across the front seat to sneak a handful of cheese popcorn while David rummaged through a backpack.

I didn't answer immediately. Inside, I knew what God was asking me to do, but it seemed so radical I just wasn't sure if I could make myself say the actual words.

Eric seemed to sense my hesitancy. He carefully opened the cap of his plastic bright-yellow bottle of Squirt, took a long swig, then looked at me.

"Do you feel like it's going to be hard to go back to high school after this week?" he ventured in a quiet voice.

I glanced out the window. A frown creased my face as I formulated my reply.

"Well," I finally said, "I guess I just feel like God may be asking me to . . . um, leave high school."

The car was silent as my words sunk in. No one laughed or looked at me incredulously as I had expected. And surprisingly, saying the words hadn't even sounded as crazy as I had thought they would.

"I've just come to the place where I have to make a choice." I continued, my voice sounding more confident with every word, "And this is a choice God has been asking me to make for a long time. I can either pursue friends and popularity and my social life at school. Or I can put all that aside and really focus on God. I've tried to fool myself into thinking I could focus on both—have friends and be popular and be a little social butterfly and still have God on the side. But He wants to be first in my life. And if I'm really going to make Him first, I have to get away from everything that distracts me from Him."

Ridgeview High School

February 1992

-leslie-

the halls were empty and filled with an eerie silence. I quietly filled my backpack with books and papers, zipped it shut and turned to close my locker one final time. As the metallic *wham* echoed throughthe still corridor, it seemed to signify the end of a season of my life. No longer was I a typical American teenager. God was calling me into a journey of radical obedience to Him. Life would never be the same. I was both terrified and excited at the same time. In spite of my fear of the unknown, not once did I question my decision. An inexplicable peace rested securely upon my heart. I knew I was doing what God wanted.

As I walked slowly out of the main entrance doors and into the deserted parking lot, a brilliant sunset greeted me. A gentle breeze stirred the trees and a surge of emotion gripped me as I gazed at the spectacular colors painting the horizon above the majestic Rocky Mountains. All at once, life was so much bigger than my meaningless little reality here at Ridgeview High. God was so much more than a concept I heard about in the youth room on Sunday nights. He was the Creator of the Universe. And He had an amazing plan in store . . . just for me.

In that moment, I felt a tender promise whispered to my soul.

I am with you. Do not be afraid of the future. I have beautiful dreams for your life, so much better than the dreams you've been chasing after for so long. Trust Me. You are my precious child and I love you so much more than you can comprehend.

leslie

Jack's Basement Studio
April 1992

-eric-

i'm sorry!" I humbly moaned into the microphone.

"That's all right!" Jack, the studio engineer, cheerfully encouraged from behind the glass. "You'll get it!"

"I've never sung harmony before," I offered—clarifying for everyone what—after nineteen takes—was already glaringly obvious.

I could see Leslie through the glass nudging Jack in the shoulder requesting the opportunity to speak into the talk-back microphone. Jack kindly moved to the side and pushed the appropriate button on the mixing console.

"Eric?" Her sweet voice echoed in my headphones, "sometimes it helps me with pitch problems to remove my headphones from one of my ears."

"Okay!" I squawked. "I'll try anything to get this line done!"

"And I know this may sound strange," she pressed on with a bit of hesitation in her voice, "but you might want to try holding your arms up above your shoulders as you sing. It seems to help with breath support."

I raised my arms up like I was preparing for crucifixion.

"Oh!" Leslie excitedly rang, "one more thing!" She giggled as she thought about what she was about to request. "I want you to try raising your upper lip, almost like a snarl to clear away your upper teeth—it helps with adding more of a treble sound."

I attempted to move my upper lip—much to the enjoyment and entertainment of all those observing in the studio that day.

"That's the idea!" Leslie cheered.

"I can't believe I'm doing this," I groaned into the microphone—headphones cockeyed on my head, arms outstretched above my shoulders, and lips rolled back demonstrating my best impression of Mick Jagger.

While everyone behind the glass was holding their stomachs and turning crimson with laughter, Jack, amidst stomach-tightening chuckles of his own, offered me one final piece of advice. "This is the look!" he bellowed. "This is it!" With a gigantic smile on his face he said, "Eric, if you're interested in finding yourself a beautiful young woman someday, this is the look that will certainly make her swoon!"

———

The studio is where I observed her. Behind glass I felt freer to watch her and study how she worked. I enjoyed seeing her artistry, her brilliant deftness with music. I enjoyed watching her argue with Jack about a note being off-pitch or not—she was always right. I enjoyed her teaching me what she knew about singing and recording—she always made it something memorable. I enjoyed finding that everything I did with her ended in laughter. Sometimes as we laughed we would catch each other's gaze and hold it for a brief moment. It was in those moments that I would complain to God and wonder why she had to be five years younger than I. This little girl named Leslie amazed me. But my thoughts were quickly disciplined and brought back into the reality of the situation. She was some other man's future treasure, and I must always treat her with that fact in mind.

Applewood Park

April 1992

—leslie—

So what kind of man do you want to marry, Les?"

My brother David and I were walking slowly along our neighborhood's winding bike path, enjoying the fresh new sights and sounds of an early spring coming to life. I sighed in contentment as we approached an apple tree full of glorious white blossoms.

Glancing sideways at David, I pondered his question with a thoughtful smile on my face. A few months ago, my brother probably wouldn't have felt comfortable asking me something this personal. It amazed me sometimes that after two years of almost completely shutting out my family, I had been able to rediscover an open, loving friendship with each one of them. My parents and brothers had been quick to forgive me, welcoming me back as an involved member of our family. And with each new day, I had begun to cherish them more and more as priceless jewels in my life.

I had been away from high school almost two months, finishing my education at home through independent study. In contrast to the social frenzy of years past, I now had very few friends my own age. But I was far from lonely or bored. God supplied my needs for companionship in His own perfect way. A few months earlier I never would have dreamed that my very best friends would become my family. Even though my brothers were still young, I was learning to relate to them as companions and confidants rather than pesky little siblings. I reached up to pick a newly budded leaf from a tree and shook my head in wonder at how different my life was now.

David had scooped up a dead twig from the ground and was absently twirling it with his thumb as we moved along. Realizing he was still waiting for an answer, I began to carefully peel the petals from the stem in my hand and think about my response.

"Um, I think more than anything, I want a man of integrity. I mean, I just want someone who is totally committed to Jesus Christ."

David tossed the twig into a nearby bush.

"Do you think it will be someone you already know, like Mark or Eric Ludy?" he questioned with the hint of a playful smile on his lips.

I laughed incredulously.

"Are you kidding? Mark and I would drive each other crazy because we're so different, and Eric . . . well, I mean . . . he's just way too old for me!"

Our conversation was momentarily halted as we were forced to the side of the path by two energetic rollerbladers. As we watched them whiz by, I added, "Besides, Eric and Mark are like two older brothers to me. And relationships with guys are not what I feel God wants me to focus on right now anyway." I swatted at a small swarm of gnats that had gathered around my head. My mind began to wander.

It still sounded strange to me every time I tried to verbalize my new attitude toward guy/girl relationships. Six months earlier, my entire existence had completely revolved around my dating world. My whole emotional state was determined by what was happening in my love life. I was obsessed with being attractive to the opposite sex, flirting at every opportunity, and pursuing relationships above all else. Relationships had been my security, my identity. Now, Jesus Christ had truly become my number one focus. Not in word only, but in the way I lived every day. And as I had slowly learned to trust Him completely as the Lord of every area of my life, I had felt His gentle challenge to my heart, *I have someone very special for you, My precious child. Wait patiently for that man, set yourself aside for him in complete purity and faithfulness. I will bring him into your life in a way more beautiful than anything you can imagine. But wait for My perfect timing. Use this time of your life to focus on Me instead of chasing after foolish, short-term pleasure.*

Faithfulness to my future husband had come to mean so much more than simply saving my virginity for him. I had made a decision, that no matter how many mistakes I had made in the past, from now on I would set myself aside in complete purity and true faithfulness for the man I would one day marry. I wanted to guard my heart, my emotions, everything. And I wanted to live in consideration of my future husband even with the guy friendships I allowed into my life. That was why I was so thankful for Eric and Mark Ludy. I was free to be their friend, knowing they were true brothers in the Lord, with no pressure or expectation that anything more would ever happen. I chuckled as I pondered David's remark. I wouldn't be marrying one of the Ludy boys, I told myself, but they were certainly out of the kind of mold I hoped God would craft my future husband when the time was right.

Chewing my lower lip thoughtfully, a fear suddenly entered my mind. *What if God brings a man of integrity into my life, and he can't see past the mistakes I've made? What if I've ruined my chances of marrying a Godly man?* I took a deep breath and forced the panic out of my heart. I probably wouldn't have to worry about something like that for several more years, I told myself firmly, determined to forget the foreboding daydream.

a s David and I wandered toward the wooden gate that led to our backyard, I heard a familiar voice behind me.

"Hey!" an out-of-breath Eric panted as he jogged up to us. Since the Ludys only lived a couple of miles away, Eric's daily running route often took him down the path behind our backyard. Beads of sweat danced on his forehead as he slowed his pace and offered us one of his friendly, ever-ready grins.

My heart beat excitedly at the sight of him. I realized every time I was with him how deeply I appreciated his friendship and how much I enjoyed being around him. He was full of energy, enthusiasm, and a tireless passion for God that never failed to inspire me in my own faith. What an amazing gift to have an older-brother friendship like this one.

My hand rested on the gate latch as I listened to Eric's animate account of a powerful prayer time he'd had that morning with his brother, kneeling together at the flagpole of my former high school (the school Mark currently attended) as the students arrived. A fleeting thought floated through my mind . . .

The girl who marries Eric Ludy will be in for the adventure of her life!

The Toyota Camry

May 1992

-leslie-

t he familiar scent of faded air freshener greeted me as I slid into the passenger's side of the red Toyota Camry and instinctively began feeling behind me for the impossible-to-find seat belt.

"So do you feel like you're learning a lot from Scott?" Eric questioned as he started the engine.

"Definitely! I've really enjoyed studying voice here—it's been amazing how much of a difference I can already see!" I replied wholeheartedly, still fidgeting for the seat belt.

Scott, Eric's lovable and incredibly gifted vocal coach, had taken me under his wing as well. Every Friday at one o'clock, Eric and I would make the drive across Denver for our "dual" voice lesson. Not only was the vocal training superb, the time Eric and I spent talking in the car each week was incredible. We would share stories of what God was doing in each of our lives, truths we had discovered while reading the Bible, and experiences from our past that had shaped us. And without fail, we would end up philosophizing about our convictions and our beliefs concerning our faith. Each week as the red Camry glided into my driveway and I said goodbye to my friend, my mind and heart were full of new ideas and thoughts to ponder. I had never in my life had such a pure, deep friendship with anyone.

"So . . . what're ya' thinking about?" Eric was looking at me curiously and I realized a soft smile had crept over my face as I thought about our friendship.

I shook my head, embarrassed. "I'm just daydreaming, I guess." I answered lightly.

Eric did not press me further. As our friendship had deepened, he was always careful to relate to me within certain boundaries. I knew he had made a commitment to be totally faithful to his future wife, even in the friendships he had with other girls. Though I knew he appreciated our companionship, I was constantly aware that he was cautious not to get emotionally involved. Though we often talked about spiritual things, Eric steered clear of venturing into anything too personal. I could tell he wanted to make sure I never got the "wrong idea" about his feelings for me. He mentioned his future wife regularly, how he was praying for her every day. The more time I spent with him, the more I realized Eric was committed to the same kind of faithfulness to his future wife as I had recently purposed to have toward my future husband. His faithful love toward her—even without knowing who she was—intrigued me.

Last week, while our families laughed together on the back porch, he and I had meandered into the living room to work on music together. We were sitting at the baby-grand piano, looking through his black spiral notebook full of lyrics to songs he'd composed, when my eye fell on one obviously written for his future wife. Fascinated, I wanted to linger on that page, to study the tender, intimate words behind the clear plastic cover sheet. But Eric had quickly flipped passed it. I briefly felt the depth of Eric's love for this woman. He treasured her, even now. He longed for the day God would bring her into his life. My heart warmed as I realized that if Eric could love his wife this way, there must be other men out there with that same kind of commitment and faithfulness. I hoped my future husband was one of them.

Secretly, I was beginning to envy Eric's future wife, wherever she was, whoever she was. To have a man like this loving her so faithfully was nothing short of a beautiful gift from heaven. The sound of Eric's voice jolted me back to the moment.

"So Les, do you mind if we stop by the Christian bookstore so I can pick up a background tape for this wedding I'm singing at?" Eric asked as he turned onto I-25 and braked for a speeding red Chevy.

"Sure, no problem," I replied. Moments later we pulled into the bookstore parking lot.

A high-pitched bell signaled as we swung open the entrance door. Stepping gingerly inside, we both began scanning the store for the music section. After a few minutes of wandering, a young man in a blue shirt and yellow tie approached us.

"Can I help you?" he asked, smiling politely. I noticed a gap in between his front teeth.

"Uh, yeah, I guess you can," Eric answered in his usual friendly style, outdoing the smile offered by the youthful clerk. "We're look-ing for a background tape to a wedding song."

"Oh, okay. The wedding section is upstairs. Why don't you just follow me?" said the clerk, already beginning to weave us through the aisle towards the winding staircase at the back of the store.

As we made our way through rows of study Bibles and com-mentaries, the young man decided to make small talk.

"So, I take it you two are getting married? Congratulations!" he boomed over his shoulder as we approached the colorful chil-dren's section.

"Uh no, actually . . . " Eric stammered awkwardly as my face began to flush. "It's uh, it's not for *our* wedding."

"Oh really?" the clerk's brows furrowed in confusion. He raised his voice to be heard above a sing-a-long video of a dancing pineapple. "So when are you two getting married?"

Eric cleared his throat nervously and was careful not to look at me. I pretended to be engrossed in studying a life-size pop-up of a well-known recording artist whose new fashion statement seemed to be a gigantic elaborate cross tattooed on his upper right shoulder.

"Um . . . no, I mean . . .we're not . . ." Eric tried to explain as our helpful salesman began jogging up the stairs.

The young man with the yellow tie was beginning to catch on.

"Oh, I see!" he said flashing the gap between his front teeth knowingly. "You're not engaged yet!"

Feeling the need to help, I jumped in. "No, we're just . . . "

Before I could say the word "friends" our overly-social clerk had interrupted.

"Well, here's the wedding section. We've got all the traditional wedding songs here, along this wall." He turned in a dramatic semi-circle and pointed to the far left corner. "And over there you'll find a lot of other wedding material," he added proudly. "We have invitations, guest books, unity candles, all that good stuff! So whenever you two set the date, make sure you check out our great selection!"

"Sure, . . . uh, . . .thanks," Eric responded weakly as the young man gave us a teasing wink and hurried away.

An hour later, my face was still burning when Eric dropped me off in front of my house.

Barb's Flowerbed

May 1992

-eric-

What are you doing right now that would possibly prohibit you from coming with us?" My mom questioned as she gestured for me to grab the first bag of mulch.

"Eric," she passionately continued while eyeing her flowerbed of the very-near-future, "I think it would be really good for you to get away."

She handed me a pair of yellow gloves and pointed to where the first bag needed to be dumped. I slipped my hands into their newfound yellow habitats then proceeded to rip the bag open in such a way that brown mulch went everywhere except the place it was supposed to go.

"To be honest," I muttered while collecting scattered chunks of the dirt-like substance, "I don't really feel comfortable spending two weeks on a 'women's getaway.' I'd be the only guy!"

My argument didn't seem to hold much water with my mom. While attacking the clumps of mulch with her rake she continued to attack me with her resolve to see me join her on her trip to Texas. "Eric Winston Ludy!" my mom stated with disciplinary fervor and a wry grin. "Since when did you start feeling uncomfortable around women?"

"I just think," I remonstrated while tossing the brown chunks into the flowerbed, "that when you get three women together, throwing a guy in the mix spoils the girl talk."

"Eric," she forcefully stated, "I don't think any of us are too worried about missing out on 'girl talk!'" Then she deviously smirked, paused from her raking, looked over at me and questioned,

"Does this have anything to do with the fact that Leslie is one of the three women?"

"Well, I think it complicates it." I retorted while reaching for the second bag of mulch.

"What do you mean it complicates it?" She continued to eye me with her maternal gaze.

"Well," I gasped, "I don't think it looks too good for me to be traveling around the countryside with this sixteen-year-old girl, visiting her grandparents and smelling blue-bonnets!" With that I busted the second bag just like the first one and mulch flew everywhere.

"Are you concerned about what others think?" Doctor Mom probed.

"Not really," I plodded. "I just don't think it's appropriate."

"Appropriate for who?" she pursued.

A few moments of silence filled the Ludy backyard as I collected dirt clods and my mom studiously perused her eldest son. Finally I confessed. "For me."

Doctor Mom moved in closer to try and diagnose her child's debilitating problem. "Do you like her?"

"No way!" I exploded. "She's just a little girl!" With that I tossed a large chunk of mulch an extra couple of feet further than was necessary and forcefully dumped the remainder of bag two into my mom's flowerbed. "I think I need to set boundaries in my life regarding how much time I spend with single members of the opposite sex."

"Eric," my mom sweetly counseled, "please don't take your stolid convictions to the point where you stop being a man able to enjoy the presence of a lady."

"I don't want to do that," I groaned while reaching for the third bag of mulch. "I guess I'm just afraid of messing up again."

"You and Leslie have been spending a lot of time together." Her eyes danced with intrigue. "Are you going to tell me that your relationship is purely platonic?"

"Purely what?" I wriggled.

"Platonic." She emphasized like only an ex-schoolteacher could. "Are you only just friends?"

"We are as plutorific as you can get!" I bellowed, having no mercy on the English language. "I don't know why everyone thinks there should be something between us!"

Once again she turned and attacked a clod of mulch, aggressively spreading it into the far eastern corner of her beloved flowerbed.

"Eric," she said while raking away, "as your mother, I think I know you quite well." She paused and looked at me to gain my agreement. Then she continued. "I don't want you to get defensive when I say this, but I think you and Leslie have a very special relationship."

"What do you mean by that?" I sheepishly muttered.

"I can tell that you really care about her," she offered.

"I do, just not like everyone thinks I do," I clarified.

"Well," she strategically expounded, "I'm proud of how you have handled the friendship, and I think your caution is honorable. I just want you to know that it wouldn't surprise me in the least if you changed your mind about liking Leslie in a way that goes beyond, as you would say, plutorific."

———

mom" talks were an essential ingredient in my childhood. I always acted as if I didn't like them, but that never stopped my mom from giving them. She was famous for using vocabulary words far too large for my pea-sized brain to handle. But even though I pretended to be confused about what she was saying, some-how I always knew exactly what message she wanted to deposit in my heart and mind.

While dumping mulch on her flowerbed in the spring of my twenty-first year, for the first time her "mom" talk genuinely con-fused me. Not because I didn't understand her choice of vocabulary words, but because she was speaking things I wasn't ready to hear.

I cared about the young girl with emerald eyes. In fact, over the past months I had caught myself thinking about her more than I felt was right and honorable. Now I found myself daily fighting to keep my thoughts pure towards her and trying not to imagine her as any-thing more than a little sister.

I was and still am a man who struggles with the sexual side of my being. But in early May of 1992 the battle's intensity rivaled something out of *Saving Private Ryan*. As I fought to keep my mind pure, I found that tattered *Playboy's* from junior high and high school still reaped vengeance on my psyche. I caught my eyes wandering in ways that were inconsiderate and dishonorable. It seemed a good portion of every day was filled with me asking God for grace and strength to live in love and purity. And time and time again I fell short and pleaded with God to wash me clean.

It's difficult being a young man in today's world and attempting to live in purity and faithfulness to your future wife. Moms are meant to be one of the few sources of inspiration and encouragement that we as young men have. As we navigate this difficult road, moms are supposed to keep us on track and help us stay far and away from the traps of the enemy.

But here was *my* mom, challenging me in one of her patented "mom" talks to possibly consider Leslie as more than just a friend. I was battling every day to do just the opposite. For twenty-one years my mom had offered me cogent and sage advice and had always been right. But now, as I ripped open the fourth bag of mulch, I was stunned by the strange realization that my mom was actually capable . . . of being wrong.

The Golden Corral
Late Springtime 1992

-leslie-

dusk was rapidly descending as our noisy group made their way from the crowded restaurant out into the muggy Texas air.

"I'm so glad Mom talked you into coming on this trip!" Krissy was saying sweetly to Eric. Krissy, Eric's lovely older sister, worked as a teacher in a missionary school near Twin Oaks ranch. Since my mom and I had already been planning to drive to Texas to visit relatives, we'd invited Eric and his mom, Barb, to join us and offered to make a stop along the way to spend some time with Krissy.

So far the trip had been a lively adventure, full of meaningless car-songs and annoying car-games (mostly invented by Eric) and frequent stops at run-down gas stations with bathrooms that looked like they had not been cleaned in at least a year.

Now that we had arrived in Tyler, we were enjoying the summer wildflowers, great country cooking, and meaningful time with Krissy.

"Oh, I am sooo full," I groaned as we approached our tan Mitsubishi Montero.

"I think I ate ten pounds of chicken," added Krissy, rubbing her stomach with a rueful giggle.

"That's why it's an all-you-can-eat buffet!" Eric exclaimed enthusiastically. "So you can chow-down til you're hurtin'!"

I smiled in amusement as I noticed a smudge of chocolate on the tip of his nose, reminding us all that in less than two minutes he had devoured a huge bowl of Oreo pudding for dessert.

"So Eric, have you and Mark decided to come back to Tyler this fall for another school?" Krissy asked as we lingered outside the car chatting and swatting at mosquitoes.

Eric gave his sister a thoughtful look. "Well Krissy, I know Marky's planning on it. But I'm, . . . well, I'm still praying about it."

Krissy studied him closely. She seemed to be able to read him so well.

"What's holding you back, Eric?" she asked quietly.

Eric shuffled his feet uncomfortably.

"I guess I just don't want to follow my own plans for my life, you know, do what I think is best without being sure it's really what God wants. I mean, I'd love to go the school, but I'm not sure about my motives." He cleared his throat, thinking about how to express his next words.

"Right now all I'm doing is studying music and it's been, . . . well, just really lonely. And I know that if I came back to Tyler this fall for the school I'd finally have close friendships in my life again. I just don't want that to be the main reason I decide to go."

Krissy nodded in understanding and began voicing another question about registration deadlines, but I could no longer concentrate on the conversation around me. A stab of pain had shot through my heart as soon as I'd heard Eric's reply. My mind reeled. *No close friends? What does he consider me? Just an acquaintance? After all the time we've spent together?*

As we piled into the cramped and stuffy car, I was thankful for the darkness. I had to fight back tears the entire way to Krissy's house. Sickened, I realized I had been totally wrong about my friendship with Eric. While I had considered him one of my closest friends, he'd just seen me as a little girl, someone he could never really relate to on a deep level. I pictured all the other friends, his own age, who would come into his life when he left for another missionary school in a few short months. It wouldn't take long before he'd forget about me completely.

I sighed in misery. Why had I let this friendship become so important to me? My heart ached to think of losing him, but the pain grew even stronger when I realized he would not feel the same way about losing me. To him, I was just another surface friend who would pass in and out of his life.

I pursed my lips together and traced an unknown pattern on the seat fabric to contain my inner turmoil. *I can't believe how stupid I've been! I thought we had a special friendship—that he really felt comfortable sharing things with me about his spiritual life that he didn't share with other people. But he probably has that kind of relationship with every friend who comes into his life! I'm no different to him than any other friend he's ever had.*

Suddenly I felt Eric's eyes on me. I attempted to look back at him as if nothing was bothering me, hoping the lack of light would conceal my pain. Up front our two mothers were chatting intently about quilting patterns. Eric was silent, watching me. I felt uncomfortable and could not meet his probing gaze. I looked out the window at the clear night sky, full of hundreds of brilliant stars. I felt small and vulnerable.

A soft whisper suddenly tickled my ear. "Give me a chance to explain Les," Eric's voice was barely audible. "Before you go inside tonight, can we talk privately?"

My heart pounded nervously. I'd never heard his voice so tender, so caring. He was genuinely affected by my pain. I could tell he was devastated at the realization that he had somehow hurt me. I nodded without looking at him.

The rest of the drive to Krissy's home, I prayed silently, *Lord, I've given You every area of my life. I don't want to cling to anything that is not of You. Eric has come to mean a lot to me, maybe too much. If you want to take away my friendship with Eric, I trust You. I know You only want what is best for me, so I surrender our entire relationship to You. Help me not to allow my emotions to lead me. May I be led only by You. Help me not try to manipulate Eric or distract him from what You are calling him to in life. But please, Lord, if this friendship is something You have put together, show me tonight in Your own special way.*

The Football Field
Late Springtime, 1992

—eric—

U h, . . ." I fumbled. "I, uh . . ."

I paused from my inarticulate murmurings to open a rickety gate for Leslie to walk through.

"Thank you." She whispered with a twinge of sadness in her voice.

We continued walking for a few minutes in total silence, led on by only the moonlight and a deep-seated awkwardness. As we rounded a wooded bend in the dirt path, we found ourselves entering a large field of grass. I spotted some bleachers and silently led my hurting friend to a place where we could sit down.

As we took a seat on the metal upholstery I again felt obligated to unskillfully mutter. "Uh, . . . I, uh . . ."

Staring into the ink-like night sky, I ached. I felt a pain that was not my own. It was as if I knew what Leslie was feeling and for some reason was able to feel it too.

"Les," I finally began, "I think I said something tonight that may have hurt you."

Leslie just sat there staring at her shirtsleeve. I ventured on.

"I guess I've been a pretty poor communicator, haven't I?" I offered.

"No," Leslie stated simply while continuing to stare at different facets of her wardrobe. "You've been fine."

"Well, maybe what I mean to say is," I paused as I tried to construct a sensible sentence, "I don't know if I've ever told you how much your friendship means to me."

There was silence while I waited for Leslie to respond. Finally she spoke. "What *does* it mean to you?"

"Les," I hesitantly expressed, "you're one of the only people in the world that I think really knows me."

Leslie shyly looked off into the starry sky. Again, moments passed in hallowed silence.

"Les, I don't think you realize how encouraging it has been to have a friend like you throughout this time I've been home in Colorado."

Leslie looked at me, a tear tenderly streaming down her cheek. "Why did you say what you did to Krissy tonight?"

I had known the very moment I spoke the words that they had wounded Leslie. I hadn't meant them the way she heard them, but whether or not I was innocent of cruel verbal assault, I *was* guilty of insensitivity to this delicate young flower.

"Les, please believe me that what I said to Krissy tonight in no way reflected upon our friendship, anymore than it would upon my friendship with my parents or my brother." I stood up and walked down a couple of bleachers to circulate the adrenaline through my body. "I know I haven't been very open in some areas of my life with you. Part of that is because I'm trying so hard to honor my future wife in all I do. I'm trying to be so careful in my relationship with you. I just don't want to do something that would hurt her."

Leslie watched me quietly, her eyes gentle and understanding, and I knew she had somehow heard what I was fumbling to express . . . that she was important to me. Until the moment when I knew I'd hurt her, I hadn't even realized just how very precious her friendship was to my life.

We sat in silence, gazing at the brilliance of the sparkling stars and listening to the insects chirp out their nightly symphony. I peeked sideways at Leslie out of the corner of my eye. She was staring into the sky, a peaceful expression on her smooth face. The breeze tugged playfully at a brown curl near her temple.

A soft ache stirred in my heart for this young flower. Suddenly I longed to reach out to her, to pull her close, to softly whisper to her just how much she meant to me.

Closing my eyes against the temptation, I sighed. I would not allow emotion to overtake me. I could not let this friendship become more than it was meant to be. I had long ago decided that I would offer my heart to only one woman ever again—my future wife. With a little ache in my heart I reminded myself that although Leslie was one of my dearest friends, she couldn't possibly be that woman . . . she was still just a little girl.

Inner-City New Orleans

July 1992

-leslie-

I'm gonna zoom, zoom, zoom around the room, room, room. I'm gonna zoom around room and praise the Lord!" About fifty cheerful little voices sang at the top of their lungs as my mom and I hesitantly entered the sweltering sanctuary. I had never helped lead a Vacation Bible School before, and working in the roughest part of New Orleans' inner-city in the stifling heat of summer made the whole endeavor a new and somewhat frightening experience.

My mom and I had arrived the afternoon before, stepping out of the airport into the smothering New Orleans summer air. We were greeted by a chorus of loud, excited cheers from the entire Ludy clan.

"I'm just so thrilled you two decided to join our ministry here this week!" Barb beamed at us. "It's going to be fun to see what God will do!"

The Ludys had kindly reserved the nicest quarters for us—a run-down apartment with only a window-unit air conditioner. My heart sank as I wondered how I could survive such suffocating heat, but I soon found out that the mission base where the Ludys were staying had only one small fan to cool five people in hundred-degree-plus weather. I made up my mind not to complain.

As I had drifted to sleep that night, I tried not to think about the cockroaches that had scurried into the corners when we flicked on the kitchen light. Surely God was going stretch me, a city-girl, through this week of new and strange discomforts.

This morning was the second day of Vacation Bible School, and as my mom and I stood uncertainly by the door, I was amazed at how excited most of the kids seemed. I had participated in Vacation Bible School when I was eight, under duress from my parents, and I couldn't remember enjoying it much at all.

As Mark led the group in a hilarious rap version of "Deep and Wide," Krissy spotted us and hurried over.

"Welcome!" she whispered with a radiant smile. I had heard from Eric that working with children was one of her greatest delights, and by the joy on her face, I could see he was right. "Why don't you two just take a seat?" she was saying, wanting to put us at ease. "After song-time, we'll have arts and crafts, and you can help us glue stovepipe whiskers on our little tinfoil mice!"

I sat in the back row and giggled as Mark entertained the hyper group of kids. A little girl with pigtails turned around and caught my eye. I gazed down at her chubby, innocent face and twinkling black eyes and smiled. She grinned sweetly back at me, revealing two missing front teeth, and I felt my heart melt. This was going to be an unforgettable week.

---

two days passed, full of what seemed like non-stop activity of singing, telling stories, coloring, gluing, and supervising. To add some diversity mid-week, the camp leaders decided to take the entire group of fifty-plus youngsters to the local park for a picnic. As I stood underneath the stone canopy, filling Dixie cups with bright red Kool-Aid, I heard a high-pitched yelp coming from the rusty swing-set a few yards away. A curly-haired little boy in brown suspenders had tumbled off the slide and was sitting on the ground holding his scraped up knee and howling as if his life depended on it.

Before I could set down my latest Dixie cup, Eric had appeared out of nowhere. He was kneeling down beside the boy, speaking soothingly to calm the hysterical child. Within seconds, the little tyke had stopped screaming and was regarding Eric with wide, solemn eyes. I watched in fascination as Eric gently scooped him up and carried him to the van, where the first aid kit was located. The whole while, he told an animated tale of "Bill Grogan's Goat" to keep the young boy's mind off his injury. A tender smile played on my lips.

Eric was a man devoted to Jesus Christ, amazingly talented in so many areas, yet humble enough to show love to even those who could never repay him. My heart began to stir with a confusing little ache. This is the kind of man I knew I wanted to spend my life with. He didn't just speak his convictions; he lived them out, even when he thought no one was watching. After seeing Eric in all kinds of settings—with his family, on car trips, on missionary ventures—there was no doubt in my mind that he was a true man of integrity. I found myself gazing after him wistfully. *If only . . .*

An icy cold splash of Kool-Aid spilled onto my hand and I realized that in my reverie I had let the Dixie cup overflow. Rolling my eyes at my carelessness, I hurriedly mopped up the sticky liquid and determined to push all thoughts of a future with Eric out of my mind. Eric was a wonderful friend and brother in the Lord. But he was such an amazing man of God, so loving and faithful toward his future wife even now . . . he deserved someone far better than me.

Tears of regret stinging my eyes, my thoughts drifted back over my past. I had made so many mistakes. So many times, I had carelessly tossed away the treasure of my heart, my purity, to young men who cared nothing about me—just for the sake of temporary gratification. I gave a bitter little laugh. Maybe if I had known there were men like Eric out there—men who valued purity and considered virtue beautiful—I wouldn't have thrown away my gift of innocence. But all I had seen were young men who seemed to cherish an "easy" girl, young men who viciously mocked anything that hinted of purity. And I had bought into the lie.

Shaking my head with remorse, I willed my raging emotions under control. Eric was leaving in a couple of short months for another missionary school in Tyler, Texas, I reminded myself quickly. He would most likely find a beautiful, virtuous woman there—someone who hadn't made the kind of relationship mistakes I had—a girl who had kept herself completely pure for her husband. After all, that was the kind of woman he was praying for every day. They would fall in love and live happily ever after serving the Lord together in some far away place like Djibouti.

I wanted to enjoy the beautiful, pure friendship we had in the time that was left, not wallow in confusion because of my growing attraction to someone who would never love me in that way.

You're not here to think about your own petty desires, Leslie, I reprimanded myself, *you are here to serve these kids.* With grim determination, I wrenched open an industrial-sized can of Jiffy to begin preparing our peanut-butter-and-jelly entree.

The rest of the week I poured myself energetically into ministry and serving. I was challenged, stretched, and encouraged deeply in my walk with God. On the last day of Vacation Bible School, as the children gathered around to give us goodbye hugs, I felt incredibly satisfied. To serve in God's kingdom, alongside people like the Ludys who lived out their faith with tireless passion, was one of the greatest joys I'd known.

As I threw my clothes into my big blue duffel bag in preparation for the trip home, I tried to fight off the ache that threatened to overtake my heart. As the end of summer loomed closer on the horizon,

I knew I would have to face the fact that Eric would be leaving soon.

Lord I know that You have a plan for this area of my life, I prayed silently. *I know You have forgiven me for my past failures. Help me not to wallow in the regret of my mistakes. You know how I feel about Eric. Right now it seems that I could never find another man like him. But I know how much he desires a future wife who has always kept herself pure. Help me focus on being a true friend to him, not dreaming about a relationship that will never happen. Help me trust You, no matter what.*

The Tan Mini-Van

July 1992

—eric—

i don't ever remember my dad crying. He was a sensitive man, but he was a sensitive man under control. The closest thing we Ludys ever saw to tearful pathos took place amidst sad movies. When the hero died a pitiful death, my dad turned into a rendition of Darth Vadar on life-support. His eyes bulged like egg yolks sunny-side-up, his lip quivered like a flag in the wind, a bassy heaving emanated from his lung cavity reminiscent of Annakin Skywalker, and his chest gyrations registered an eight on the Richter scale. But he never cried.

When I was young and impressionable in my maleness, I learned that tears equated to timidity—crying equated to "Cry Baby!" So all growing up I had learned to stuff my feelings inside and cloak my pain with things other than sobs. When I watched a sad movie, I didn't sound like Darth Vadar. No! Instead, I found myself laughing uncontrollably.

For years I had stopped-up the river of feeling—I guess maybe it was only a matter of time before the dam finally broke. But I never would have expected it to break when it did.

———

yeah, put that one in!" I excitedly chirped as Leslie filed through our collection of audiotapes. "I don't know if I've ever heard it."

"This is one of my favorites!" Leslie pronounced as the Twila Paris tape was eagerly swallowed up by the van's stereo unit. "I can't believe you've never heard it before."

After a matter of seconds the musical adventure began. The mood was created, the atmosphere defined.

"Oh!" I chastised myself. "I've heard this before."

"I listen to this all the time while I study," Leslie added to clarify her appreciation for what we were about to hear.

I knew it was time to speak. For the last two days of our New Orleans mission outreach, I had painfully wrestled with the reality of my error. Deep within I knew I had fumbled my responsibility towards my future wife. Now, as our group ambled home to Colorado in the spacious tan mini-van, I knew I needed to rectify my mistake. I just had no idea how I should do it. Everyone was sleeping in the back of the van, Leslie and I were alone in the front. The music was playing just loud enough to cover up our conversation—now was obviously the time to confront the awkward issue.

"Uh, . . ." I floundered as the music tinkled in my ears. "Les?"

Leslie turned toward me. I searched my mind for how to say what I needed to say.

"I don't know how to say this," I uncomfortably groaned, "but I'm concerned about our friendship."

It was a strange sensation. I could feel Leslie immediately put up a protective wall around her heart. I somehow knew what she was feeling. And I also somehow knew that I had already hurt her delicate heart.

Lord, please help me! I silently muttered heavenward. I allowed a few moments to pass then I attempted to redeem myself.

"Les?" I stammered while nervously thumping my thumb against the steering wheel. "I care about you deeply, and that is why I am concerned."

She subtly turned her body towards the passenger side window and absently stared into the darkness.

"Let me explain what I mean," I softly pleaded.

I took a pause to figure out exactly what I did mean. Then I carefully continued.

"God has called me to treat you and honor you like a sister." I adjusted my bottom in my seat and proceeded. "I want you to discover His highest and best for your life. I want you to be set apart for His purposes and not distracted by other things. I feel it is my duty as an older brother in your life to protect His interests for you."

Again I paused, took a couple of deep breaths, studied oncoming headlights for a few rugged moments, and then charged back into the emotional battle.

"I also feel strongly, and I know this may not make total sense to you, but . . . I really want to live in a manner that, if my future wife were watching me, she would feel honored and adored."

I glanced over at Leslie, who was still forlornly staring out the side window. A deep pang stabbed at my heart.

"Les," I stumbled onward, "I want to also honor *your* future husband. I want to treat you in a manner, that if he could see, would let him know that I am caring for you and not competing with him for your heart and time."

Then with a subtle change to the tone of my voice, I whispered, "He's going to have to be one amazing man to deserve you!"

A tiny smile creased Leslie's sweet face and her eyes gently nodded her acceptance of my comment.

"When I say I'm concerned, what I mean is I feel that maybe we should take a step back from our friendship and imagine how our future spouses would feel if they were to come into our lives right now. Would they feel comfortable with all the time we are spending together? For instance, would your future husband even have a shot at winning your heart with an old guy like me constantly hanging around, vying for your time and attention?"

Leslie carefully began to turn her body, her facial features now a bit more interpretable. The music still playing, but neither one of us was conscious of its ebbs and flows.

"I guess what I'm trying to say is, I care about you too much, and I care about my future spouse too much, to not bring this issue up and address it."

With that Leslie turned and faced the conflicted driver. Her eyes were soft with understanding and her lips were smiling with appreciation. All she said was, "Thanks!"

As she spoke, one song faded out to silence and the next song began. As this change in dynamic occurred something profoundly tender touched my heart. It was a penetrating sensation I had never before felt. It weakened me. It stripped me of the protective emotional guard I had strategically built throughout my life. All I could get out were six words. And even those barely escaped.

"I really do care about you!" I haltingly spoke. Then it was as if something powerfully supernatural closed my mouth and broke the dam within my heart. As the song played, I cried—like I never have before. Deep sobs welled up from somewhere within me and ushered forth a river of tears—which were totally unfamiliar to my cheeks.

Embarrassed, I attempted to control myself, but it was like trying to stop a tidal wave with a toothpick. Leslie just watched as I cried, not knowing quite what to think, but clearly knowing God was present in an amazing way.

All we could do as I wept was listen to the music emanating from the dash board speakers. The words poignantly stirred my heart and mind. The irony was too great for human manufacturing. The words spoke of Jesus Christ and His love for His future bride. The song surged with how profoundly and deeply our Lord cherishes and adores His spouse. That song, entitled *How Beautiful*, served as the background for one of the most amazing spiritual encounters with God I have ever experienced. And there was Leslie, serving as a witness to this unforgettable episode of emotion. She was just a young girl—but this young girl now knew me like precious few did.

The tears were never mentioned. When the song concluded Leslie was gracious to act as if it had never occurred. For quite some time we sat staring out the front windshield, silently pondering what should be said next. After several unsuccessful attempts to speak, I finally made my first sound.

"I think I need to talk with your dad," I heralded.

Internally my heart skipped a beat and my blood grew chilly as I heard myself speak those words. My mind had a thought, but my lips had betrayed my mind and spoken something that sounded romantically incriminating. In the culture in which I was raised, dads are only talked to for one reason, and one reason at all—to ask for a daughter's hand in marriage. And under absolutely no circumstances would that have been my intention with those words. I simply felt her dad could provide me with some advice as to how Leslie and I could be more careful in our friendship. I certainly did not mean I wanted to ask for her hand!

Before I could alter my blundering remark, Leslie countered with, "I think you should too!"

While both of us turned shades of red that would have made a ripe tomato jealous, neither of us was aware of the significance of our verbal miscues. While we both shifted in the front seats of the tan mini-van, speeding 67 mph down the Texas interstate toward Amarillo, little did we know that the stage was being set for a conversation that would change my life.

Part Three:

the love story

Mexican Carry-Out

July 1992

-leslie-

i pushed back the lacy white curtain from my bedroom window and stared down at the grainy pavement in front of our house. A grin crept across my face as I spotted Eric in the red Toyota Camry turning onto Rambling Rose Road, making his way toward our front curb. Checking my appearance quickly in the ornate mirror above my dresser, I hurried downstairs to greet him.

"Bye mom!" I called as I grabbed my vocal notebook and jacket. "See you in a few hours!"

I jerked open the front door and found myself staring into the rich brown eyes and irresistible smile I had come to know so well.

"Hey!" Eric said in his typical enthusiastic way. Was it just my imagination, or was there something different in his manner toward me? As we made our way down the front walk to where the Camry was waiting, there was a brief moment of awkwardness. I bit my lower lip in thought. Our friendship had never been strained or awkward. But lately, strange things had been happening. Our last conversation had been exactly one week ago, in the tan mini-van on the way home from New Orleans. We had both agreed to take a week apart and seek God's heart about our friendship.

Now it was Friday afternoon, time for our weekly vocal lesson with Scott. Eric had called me that morning with a hesitant request.

"I know this sounds like a funny thing to ask Les," he had stammered, "but I have to be in a wedding rehearsal down in Boulder right after voice lessons. Would you mind coming with me? It should only take an hour or so."

"Uh, well, are you sure the bride and groom don't mind a total stranger watching their rehearsal?" I replied uncertainly.

"Oh not at all!" he had assured me, "I checked with them and they'd love to have you."

So here I was, dressed up for a wedding rehearsal and trying to conceal how glad I was to be with Eric again after what seemed like six very long days.

Nothing was said about our friendship. We didn't mention the praying we had both done that week about each other. Neither one of us really knew how to bridge the gap into that uncomfortable territory. But as we sped west on I-70 towards Wadsworth, I could tell there was more on Eric's mind than he was letting on, and I was pretty sure that his preoccupation somehow involved me. I just wasn't sure what he was thinking. My mind raced with possibilities. Maybe he'd been convicted by God as he prayed that our friendship was wrong and we couldn't spend any more time together. Maybe he'd decided to leave immediately for a missionary venture in Turkey and was searching for a gentle way to tell me. I tried hard to hide my inner turmoil as we pulled up in front of the music studio.

Voice lessons progressed as usual. Eric became his typical energetic self again. Everything seemed back to normal until, about an hour later, we found ourselves sitting side by side in a quaint wedding chapel as the bride and groom rehearsed their vows for the ceremony.

"Okay," the smiling pastor was telling the jittery wedding party, "after the unity candle, then Julie will walk over to that microphone and sing her song."

A pretty young woman, presumably one of the bridesmaids, took her cue and positioned herself in front of the wobbly microphone stand as the pianist shuffled sheet music and began to pump out a melodious accompaniment.

I had been transfixed by the gorgeous patterns on the stained glass windows, not paying much attention to the practicing up on stage. Yet with the first words the smiling brunette sang, my heart leapt into my throat and my eyes grew wide with disbelief. It was *How Beautiful!* The very same melody Eric had wept to during our unforgettable talk on the drive home from New Orleans one week earlier! I ventured a quick glance at Eric out of the corner of my eye. He was staring straight ahead as if he hadn't noticed anything unusual. But he was careful not to look at me.

Throughout the remainder of the song, I chided myself. *Don't be so stupid, Leslie! It's just a weird coincidence. Eric probably doesn't even remember that it's the same song!*

I stole another peek at Eric. This time I was almost sure I could see a glimmer of unshed tears dancing in his eyes. His hands trembled slightly and I realized he was working hard to contain a well of emotion the music had called up inside of him.

He's thinking of his future wife, I told myself, *he knows that in order to be faithful to her now he will have to end his friendship with me.*

While I deeply admired such commitment on his part to the woman he would one day marry, I couldn't stop the flood of heartache that filled me as I made this discovery.

So that's what was on his mind when he picked me up today! No wonder he didn't know how to say it!

I sat numb and unmoving during the rest of the rehearsal. Eric was called up to sing his song—another piece about true love and commitment that made my heart sink even further.

Why did you allow this friendship to come into my life, Lord, I pleaded internally, *if you only meant to take it from me so ruthlessly!*

Trust Me was the only answer that came creeping softly into the caverns of my mind. Absently I studied the worn hymnal wedged in the wooden holder in front of me. Suddenly my eye caught sight of a tall figure standing in front of me, waiting for me to notice him. It was Eric.

"Oh hi, um yeah, that was really . . . um, really good up there," I stuttered, hoping he couldn't read the conflict on my face.

He smiled at me in a tender way, saying nothing for a few seconds— which caused my discomfort to grow even more. I shifted awkwardly in my seat.

"Listen Les, do you want to go grab some Mexican food on the way home?" he offered, completely taking me off guard.

"Oh, well, yeah, sure, I guess so." I seemed incapable of concise, articulate answers at the moment.

He's taking me out to dinner so he can break the news to me gently, I thought miserably as we said our goodbyes and nice-to-meet-yous to the wedding party and took our leave.

———

Thirty minutes later we were seated on a huge boulder overlooking a breathtaking view of the valley below. A styrofoam take-out container dripping with cheese and hot sauce was balanced precariously on my lap.

"So Les," Eric began, pausing momentarily to carefully spear a bite of chicken enchilada with his flimsy plastic fork, "what do you think God has done in your life over the past few months through our friendship?"

My heart began to flutter nervously. It was the first time any mention of our relationship had been spoken of since the tan van conversation a week ago. I wasn't sure what to say. My eyes searched the valley below, as I tried to summon up words to adequately express everything this friendship had come to mean to me.

I took a long slurp from my diet Coke to stall for time as Eric waited patiently for a reply.

"This friendship has meant so much to me," I began, inwardly groaning at how cliché my words sounded to my own ears. I tried again. "I mean, I really feel God has used you in my life to draw me nearer to Him. And you've been like a wonderful older brother in my life. I consider you one of my closest friends."

I could feel my face flush with embarrassment at the honesty of my words. Eric didn't seem to notice. He nodded thoughtfully, scooping up the remainder of his enchilada sauce with a soggy tortilla chip.

"I know what you mean," he conceded, attaching the lid of his take-out dish securely in place. "It sometimes amazes me that one of my best friends could be a sixteen-year-old girl. But Les, you know me in a way very few people do. And you understand me in a way very few people do." Eric began to gather up the remains of our Mexican feast into a white plastic bag brimming with unused paper napkins. I looked on silently, my heart a little lighter after hearing that my friendship was still so valuable to him.

After a few seconds of rummaging, Eric turned to face me. "Les," he said softly, his voice thick with emotion, "I don't know what God's plans are for this friendship. I want to take the rest of this weekend and continue praying about it. And I want you to keep praying about it, too. But no matter what happens I just want you to know . . ." he hesitated, distractedly brushing a layer of gravel and sand off his leather shoe as he searched for the right words, "I just want you to know that you are very special to me and nothing is ever going to change that."

he "goodbye speech" I had been anticipating never came. On the forty-five minute drive home, little was said. Yet there was a silent peace filling the car. A weight lifted off my chest and my heart felt free. No questions were answered, no problems were solved, no conclusion was reached. But I was special to Eric. Nothing was going to change that. And for tonight, I decided as he eased the Toyota Camry into my driveway and I slowly gathered up my things, that was really all I needed to know.

Perkin's Family Restaurant

July 1992

-eric-

hiya!" The matronly woman shouted. "My name's Margie and I'll be your server! Can I start you out with some drinks?" And with that she resumed smacking her exhausted wad of gum.

"Just coffee," Rich Runkles casually remarked, then resumed his perusal of the menu.

"Margie," I smiled, "I'll be fine with water."

"Sure ya don't wan' any coffee, hon?" She kindly questioned.

"No thanks!" I stated as she reached across the table to remove my upside down coffee mug.

Adrenaline was pumping through my wiry body already; the last thing I needed was another stimulant. I studied my menu as if I were preparing for a final exam on country skillets, the whole while wondering how I was going to talk with the cream-and-sugarless coffee drinker across the table.

The next couple of minutes were full of small talk about the Sunday morning sermon, the conspiratorial shrinkage of portions restaurants serve nowadays, and peripheral ramblings with Margie about Rich's order of some chicken salad thing and my order of a Southwestern skillet.

At about one thirty-seven on that never-to-be-forgotten Sunday afternoon, I finally spoke something of substance.

"Rich," I hesitantly muttered, "I'm concerned about my friendship with Leslie." It was a strategic statement intended to clarify my intentions of getting together with him. Not for a moment did I want him to think I was actually interested in his daughter in a romantic way. I figured the word "concerned" would definitely reveal to him my true objectives.

The next few minutes were filled with my ramblings about my desire to honor my future wife and Leslie's future husband. I provided a wonderful opportunity for Rich to correct me and chastise me for overstepping boundaries with his daughter. But he did no such thing. When I finally took a breath, Rich spoke.

"Eric," he carefully chose his words, "do you know the reason that I know you're friendship with my daughter is of God?"

I stared at him dumbfounded and raised my eyebrows as a show of interest.

"Well Eric," he continued, "it's because ever since you have come into her life, I have seen her grow closer to Jesus Christ."

I formed my lips as I prepared to respond, but Rich quickly interjected his next thought.

"And do you know why I am certain your relationship with my daughter is pure?" He paused for effect why I swallowed hard and loosened my shirt collar—again raising my eyebrows as if to say "Uh, . . . no . . . (gulp) . . .why?"

"Because if it wasn't," he eyed the curly-headed young man across the table from him and finished with conviction, "God would show me!"

As the afternoon crept on, Margie reconnoitered my water glass every three minutes to help create the illusion that I was sipping from a bottomless well. She was also quick to refuel Rich with the necessary caffeine for our discussion. It wasn't but every seven minutes we would encounter a lull in conversation. I would pick at my napkin and take sips from my glass of ice water to try and occupy the empty space, but after thirty seconds or so the conversation would start back up. It was strange for me to have a lunch engagement with someone my parents' age. I was insecure and anxious, but this tender man somehow made me feel loved and accepted.

I felt understood. I felt like this gentle man had heard my heart and had encouraged me in return. It wasn't until after Margie slipped our meal bill under Rich's eager left hand that he began to act a little funny. Right as we were preparing to get up from our booth, Rich offered one final addendum to our discussion.

"Eric," he began, "I give you my blessing to pursue a relationship with my daughter in any way that God would lead you."

I choked on my final bite of chocolate cream pie. "Uh," I floundered, "Rich, I thought you realized that I'm not interested in pursuing a relationship like that with Leslie!"

Placidly, and without even a blink, he looked me in the eye and stated, "I know, Eric." Then with the certitude that only comes with knowing the God of the Universe he calmly articulated, "I just felt like I needed to express that to you."

311 Rambling Rose Road

July 1992

—leslie—

i paced nervously around the kitchen, my eyes glued expectantly to the wooden door leading into the house from the garage.

"What's taking him so long?" I muttered in frustration as I began another agitated lap around the center island chopping block.

My mom glanced up from a cookbook photograph of a brilliantly colored strawberry pie. She studied me quizzically.

"What's wrong with you, Les?"

I sighed impatiently.

"I just can't stand not knowing what Eric is talking to Dad about!" I complained loudly. "I mean, Eric and I agreed to take the rest of the weekend to keep praying about our friendship. But I haven't heard from Eric in two days. And now he and Dad have been out together for almost two hours and I want to know what's going on!"

"Well, why do *you* think Eric wanted to get together with Dad?" My mom's curiosity had been piqued as well. She began rummaging in the refrigerator for a carton of fresh strawberries as she waited for my reply.

"I have no idea!" I shook my head. "All I know is that we both feel that we really need to be careful in our friendship and I know Eric's really concerned about honoring his future wife."

"So Eric getting together with Dad is not because he wants to move beyond a friendship with you?" My mom eyed me carefully as she dumped a handful of berries into a bright blue colander.

I could feel heat creeping into my face and quickly opened the pantry door, gazing at the meager selection of crackers and soup cans to hide my embarrassment.

"No! I mean, that would be impossible," I stammered awkwardly, reaching for a half-eaten bag of Ritz. "Believe me, no matter how good friends we are, I'm not the kind of girl he wants to spend the rest of his life with!" I gave a sarcastic little laugh.

"What do you mean by that?" My mom stopped what she was doing and looked at me with interest. I shoved a crumbly cracker into my mouth and shrugged.

"Well, his standards for what he wants in a wife are really high," I informed her, brushing crumbs off my face. "And, he's been so faithful to his future spouse. He prays for her every night!" My voice rang with admiration.

"So . . . " my mom was staring at me in confusion.

"So, what?" I prompted.

"So, I still don't understand why you don't think he would be interested in you," she said with conviction, cracking two eggs over a bowl.

I sighed and studied the intricate pattern on the cracker in my hand. "I don't know . . . I guess I just think he deserves someone better than me!" I finally blurted out.

"Leslie," my mom's voice proclaimed, "just because you've made mistakes in your past, doesn't mean it's too late for you to find a real man of God to marry!"

I eyed her skeptically. "Well, sometimes I just wonder if I've ruined my chances for a fairy tale," I confessed. "I mean, I used to have so many dreams of a knight in shining armor and riding off into the sunset . . ." my voice trailed off as I sighed sadly. "And then, when I got older and saw a little more of the world, I stopped believing that Prince Charming even existed. Until . . . until I met Eric." My voice grew soft and reflective with the words. I turned back to stare vacantly into the still-open pantry and continued baring my soul.

"I just think that now it's too late for me. I know God's forgiven me for what I did, but . . . I know I don't deserve someone like Eric." I paused and shut my eyes for a moment before whispering, "I know he would never want someone like me."

My mom was silent and thoughtful as she began slicing ripe, juicy strawberries on a cutting board.

"Leslie," she finally responded, "don't limit what God wants to do in this relationship with Eric. God is not holding your past sins over your head. He has removed them from you as far as the east is from the west—just like the Bible says!" She looked up at me with eyes full of compassion and stated, "And don't underestimate what God can do in Eric's heart if He has meant for you two to be together! You've been waiting faithfully for the right man ever since God changed your life. You may be exactly the kind of pure and virtuous woman Eric Ludy has been praying for!"

S o?" I questioned, a bit too eagerly. "What did Eric want to talk to you about?" My dad had just walked into the house from his meeting with Eric, an unreadable expression on his face. I held my breath as he reached for a Ritz and popped it into his mouth, chewing slowly and swallowing before answering my breathless question.

"Les, I really think you should let Eric talk to you about it."

"Why? Was it something bad? Like he never wants to see me again?" I interrogated with intense urgency.

My dad smiled gently and shook his head, biting into another cracker.

"No, it wasn't anything bad at all." His calm reply only served to make my agitation all the more obvious. He glanced at my mom who was busily whipping two egg yolks with a fork. "I'm going up to change clothes," he informed us mildly, and headed out of the kitchen.

With a frustrated groan, I lowered myself onto a stool and rubbed my temples.

"Don't worry, Les," my mom comforted, setting the oven to 325°. "I'm sure Eric won't leave you hanging much longer. He's one of your closest friends. I know he's not just going to disappear out of your life."

I nodded quietly, a resigned expression on my face. As I gazed distractedly out the screen door at the hanging flower basket on the back porch, I wondered why Eric Ludy's conversation with my dad was so urgently important to me. If he was only a good friend like I kept telling myself, why did my heart do somersaults whenever I thought about him?

Lord, I guess I'm going to just have to keep trusting You. I spoke silently to the sky. *I don't know how Eric feels about me. Maybe he wants to end this friendship altogether. But I know You will be faithful, no matter what. Help me be patient until Eric decides to tell me how he feels about this friendship. Help me trust You.*

1422 South Newport Way

August 3rd, 1992

—leslie—

hey Les! Look at this!" Eric proudly held up a tattered spiral notebook with childish scribbles decorating the cover.

I glanced up from the packets of baseball cards I was sorting through and raised my eyebrows with amusement.

"Okay," I asked teasingly, "what amazing treasure have you uncovered this time?"

"Les!" he chastised solemnly, "this is my first published work!"

I leaned forward to study the dilapidated cover with the scrawled words, "The Adventures of Garfield and Santa Claus." I raised my head, genuinely curious now.

"It's a novel my buddy Kevin and I collaborated on in the second grade!" Eric proclaimed, beaming with memories. "I drew the pictures, and Kevin wrote the story!" He thumbed through the notebook, displaying each of the elaborate cartoons. "Our teacher thought it was so good that she placed a copy of it in the Oak Park Elementary School library for people to check out! I bet it's still there to this very day!"

Before I could congratulate him on his huge literary success, a knock sounded on the door and Mark poked his head in.

"How's the trunk-cleaning goin'?" he wanted to know. "Hey! Where did you get that Luke Skywalker action-figure? That was mine!" He snatched up the battered toy and examined it with enthusiasm.

"Marky, look at all this stuff we're finding!" Eric exclaimed, ignoring his brother's indignant outburst. He pointed around the room at hundreds of sentimental treasures. "You should clean out your trunk, too! You never know what's in there after all these years!"

I nodded in agreement. "You know, it was so great of your mom to start a treasure trunk for you guys when you were little!" I observed. "One day your kids are going to love going through all this!"

"That's true!" Mark agreed. "But there's no way I have time to clean out my trunk right now. I still have to buy a pair of hiking boots for the trip to Tyler. See you two later!" He tossed the Luke Skywalker back into its pile and left the room, whistling loudly.

Eric rolled his eyes. "Marky must be changing his ways. He doesn't usually pack for anything until the day he's leaving!"

My smile faded at his words as I was again reminded that Eric and Mark would be leaving for their five-month missionary venture in just a few short weeks. I had been trying not to think about it lately, but in the back of my mind, the cloud of Eric's departure loomed closer with each passing day.

Ever since that talk we'd had in the tan van on the drive home from New Orleans, I had been diligently praying about my friendship with Eric. At first, I'd been expecting God to speak to me a message of correction, to let me know that I needed to back away from this amazing friendship in order to honor my future husband and be considerate of Eric's future wife. But surprisingly, no correction had come. The more I prayed, the more peace I felt about the friendship. If there had been any message spoken to my heart from God it had been . . . *this friendship is a gift I have given you, a treasure I have brought into your life. I am smiling upon this.*

In addition to feeling such peace when I prayed about the friendship, new emotions had begun to take root in my heart toward Eric. Eric had still not bridged the gap of talking about what he felt God's will was for our friendship. But in spite of not knowing how he felt, my feelings of attraction and affection toward him were growing at an alarming rate. Other than the brief conversation I'd had with my mom

leslie

a few days earlier, I was afraid to tell anyone how I really felt about Eric, or even to write the thoughts in my journal. This was mostly because I was sure Eric did not feel the same way toward *me*. But at night, as I drifted off to sleep, I would sometimes allow myself to imagine what it would be like to spend the rest of my life with this man named Eric Ludy. And when I did, I would fall asleep with a smile and incredible contentment flooding my heart at the very thought.

W hat's on your mind?" Eric's words suddenly made me jump. I looked up, startled, reminding myself with great relief that he could not read my thoughts.

"I guess I'm just thinking about you guys leaving for Tyler in a couple of weeks," I smiled sadly. "It's going to be hard to see you go."

"Yeah," he agreed softly, a far away look in his eyes. "Yeah, it will be really hard to leave."

We worked silently for a few minutes, the air heavy with unspoken feelings.

"Les," Eric's voice came crashing through the quiet, "there is so much I want to say to you. But . . . I just want to be careful of the timing. I mean, until I'm sure what God wants . . . I just can't . . ." his voice trailed off. I gazed at him, trying to read the tormented expression on his face.

"I understand," I told him quietly, but deep inside I wondered if I really did.

"Hellooo." Barb's cheerful voice sing-songed its way down the hall. "Do you two want some left-over tuna surprise casserole?"

The emotion in the room evaporated as quickly as the steam from a hot bath.

Eric cleared his throat and attempted to make his voice sound lighthearted. "Yeah sure, we'll be right down!"

"I probably should go after lunch," I told him as I cautiously slipped rubber bands around my perfectly stacked piles of baseball cards. "I have a worship meeting at two at the church."

Eric nodded, saying nothing. I glanced up and caught his gaze. Our eyes met for one instant of silent understanding. Things were changing between us, of that much I was certain. But in that moment I could never have known just how dramatic the change would become over the next few days.

1422 South Newport Way
Eric's Bedroom
August 3, 1992

-eric-

i noticed my windowsill was a little dusty as I stared out through the double-paned glass, pondering my life. A young girl was climbing into her car, buckling her seat belt, and turning on the ignition. I secretly watched as this beautiful young girl carefully pulled out of the Ludy driveway, avoiding a red-headed pedestrian walking a red-headed dog. As she disappeared around the Newport Way bend, I thought about my wife. I prayed for her every day, wrote her love letters and even a few love songs. I didn't know what she would be like, in nature, character, demeanor, and beauty. But I found myself asking God that if there was another young woman in the world who resembled Leslie—both on the inside and outside—I wanted Him to set her aside for me.

Why does she have to be so young? I silently ached.

Suddenly in my wonderings, I noticed my sister walking down the hallway.

"Krissy?" I shouted.

After a few moments her smiling face appeared around my doorframe. "Yes?" she enthusiastically responded.

Awkwardly, with reddening cheeks, I uttered, "Could . . . uh . . . I talk with you for a second?"

"Sure!" she cheered.

The next hour passed like a hiccup attack in the middle of a wedding ceremony. It was painfully clumsy and gawky but precisely what I needed to settle my heart and mind.

While sitting next to her on the carpeted floor, I groaned out the frustration and confusion that had been stuffed inside my heart for months.

"She's too young!" I bantered.

"Why do you say that?" she bantered back.

"Isn't it obvious?" I questioned.

"Why is age such a sensitive issue?" she questioned back.

I fidgeted, I floundered, I fumbled, and I fought. But still in the end all I could muster was the truth. "Krissy . . . I can't get her off my mind. When I pray for my wife, I find myself praying for her too. And what bothers me the most is that it seems like everything that has happened in my life since I met her points toward something."

"What do you mean by *something?*" Krissy mercilessly interrogated.

"Something! You know!" I stammered.

"No I don't," she played coy. "You'll have to explain."

I took a deep breath. "I'm scared that God has something more in mind for our relationship and that I can't accept something more."

"You mean you wouldn't want there to be something more?" Krissy carefully probed.

"No, that's not what I mean," I squirmed. "But for some reason I can't accept it." A dramatic pause filled the air while I pulled at the carpet nap and studied its resilience to torture. Then with the finality of a fat lady's song I squawked, "She's just too young!"

"Do you wish she were older?"

I thought about Krissy's question for some time. I had previously mused that having Leslie be just a few years older would have solved every problem, but now as I thought about this young girl I found myself mystified with the reality of my own emotions.

"Just think, Eric!" Krissy excitedly whispered, "if it were God's plan for you and Leslie to spend your lives together, what a privilege it would be to have had the opportunity to see her grow up."

As Krissy left that day, I once again returned to my dusty windowsill. I stared out at the world that could never possibly understand my convictions, my confusions, and my considerations for this young woman named Leslie.

Show me, Lord! Show me what your will is!

Perkin's Family Restaurant
August 22, 1992

-eric-

rich sipped at his coffee, I slurped at my ice water. At five-thirty in the morning, while most of the world was picking at their alarm clocks trying to find the snooze buttons, Rich and I were picking at our omelets trying to figure out a way to start our conversation.

Rich coughed a couple times but that didn't seem to help. I cleared my throat but that only brought Hal, our waiter, to our table to ask if everything was all right.

"I, uh," I started.

Rich's eyes rose above the rim of his coffee mug with great interest. Then when I said, "I'm glad you could make it this morning," he realized we still hadn't gotten anywhere.

"It was no problem at all," he kindly remarked.

"I, uh," I once again muttered. Then still uncomfortable to bridge the real issue, I concluded, "I think we're becoming regulars here at Perkin's, don't ya think?"

Rich chuckled. But still awkwardness filled our booth.

By the time I stammered, "I, uh," for the third time, Rich wasn't hanging on my every word. But it was on the third try I finally got the "real issue" out.

"I, uh, think that God has shown me, Rich, that Leslie one day will be my wife."

I did it! I said the impossible! It wasn't a quote I would want to put on my refrigerator, but it got the job done. And it sure did catch Rich a little off guard. He took a few minutes to compose himself and make sure he hadn't spilled coffee all over the front of his tie.

I slurped my ice water like a man finding a water fountain in the middle of the Sahara. Rich took a few more sips from his coffee mug. Then he spoke.

"Eric," he carefully chose his words, "Janet and I have been praying for Leslie's future husband every day for the past fourteen years, since we became Christians." Then catching my gaze with his gentle eyes he said a collection of words from the English language I will certainly never forget: "And we have both felt, for some time now, that *you're the one!*"

The Ludy Kitchen
August 26, 1992

-eric-

Okay, I'm going to be blunt," I stated with confidence. "What in the world is going on?"

The pepperoni pizza was almost gone and it was time to get down to business.

"What do you mean?" my dad warmly responded.

"I mean," I vocalized with great passion in my voice, "I have never seen a relationship like this in my entire life. What is going on?"

"Eric," Rich kindly offered, "I don't know if you're going to like my answer, but I honestly don't know."

"Eric," my dad added, "often God does things in our life that may not fit *our* grid of 'normal.' What He's doing between you and Leslie is not something I totally understand either. But 'normal' to God isn't a set formula, it's obedience no matter what the cost, absolute trust in His leading, and total dependence upon Him for the outcome."

"I agree," Rich comforted, "God is up to something Eric, in your life and in Leslie's. It is obvious to both your dad and me. We may not understand what God is doing, but we do know that He is active in this relationship and He is going to build it in his own perfect way. And like Win is saying, we all need to trust Him and move forward, believing He will lead and guide."

Between slices of pepperoni and swigs of Pepsi, sagacious words were wrapped up in nice little understandable packages and transferred from my two fathers into my heart and mind. These men knew me and cared about me, and they both desired that I would discover God's highest and best.

During one of our conversational lulls, my dad picked up the pizza boxes and stuck them by the door leading out to the garage. He asked us both if we wanted hot tea or coffee. "I'll have some coffee," Rich eagerly responded.

"I'm fine," I said.

When my dad sat down after filling up his "Dads are Great" mug with piping hot peppermint tea and filling up Rich's "Grand Tetons" mug with cream and sugarless coffee, we were ready to really get serious.

"I think we should pray." Rich declared matter-of-factly.

"Let's do it!" My dad agreed.

Two hands stretched out towards me and rested gently on my shoulders. And two men asked God on my behalf for wisdom, direction, grace, patience, and blessing upon what was still yet to come.

"Father," my dad reverently prayed, "may Eric and Leslie discover You in a more intimate way than they ever even believed was possible."

"And Lord," Rich added, "may all of us have Your supernatural wisdom to know how and when to take steps forward. None of us are sure about what You are doing, but all of us are certain that You have initiated this relationship. Bless Eric for the manner in which he has approached this friendship with my daughter. Bless him for how he has honored me, her father."

"And bless him," my dad echoed, "for how he has honored me, his own father."

A chorus of "amens" eventually rang, and all of us returned to our pre-prayer positions.

"Thanks," I humbly said. "Thank you so much!"

If I didn't know better I would have thought my dad had tears in his eyes. But before I could investigate, Rich spoke up.

"Eric," he calmly stated, "have you spoken to Leslie about how you feel?"

"No," I responded. "I didn't want to do anything until I had a chance to talk with both of you."

"I think that was wise," Rich said. "It is always better to err on the side of being too slow than too fast when a woman's heart is concerned. But I think she is ready to hear what is taking place in you."

Then he continued with a very pensive yet pleasant look on his face, "Eric, this may sound strange, but I say this in all seriousness and with the conviction that the words I'm about to say hold value before God in heaven. As Leslie's father, I want to give you my blessing . . . to win my daughter's heart."

Applewood Park

August 26, 1992

-leslie-

h ow 'bout here?" Eric pointed to a flat spot on the top of the little hill we had approached. Shrugging my assent, I sank down onto the lush carpet of freshly cut grass and breathed deeply, savoring the warm August air.

He positioned himself across from me, flicking an ant from his jeans before looking up at me with an eager grin.

Inwardly, I was trembling, but I tried my hardest to give an outward front of confidence as I picked absently at chunks of grass and waited for him to begin speaking.

"I have something important I want to talk to you about," he had told me on the phone that morning. "Can we meet later and take a walk or something?"

My heart had hammered in my chest as I had quietly agreed to meet him at one o'clock in a nearby park. Was he finally going to tell me the friendship was over?

Secretly, I wondered if he had somehow been able to see inside my heart and discover the way I felt about him. *Maybe that's the reason he wants to end things between us before the friendship progresses any further,* I had tormented myself. *He can read my mind, he knows how I feel, and he wants to put a stop to it before he has to break my heart!*

Now, as I sat across from him, I did my best to brace myself for what was inevitably coming. As Eric took a deep breath to signify a long soliloquy, I was flooded with dread.

I hugged my knees and stared at him with a stoic expression.

"God's fingerprints have been all over this relationship from the very beginning," he spoke, his voice low and intense with meaning. "I couldn't always see it, but now looking back, it seems so obvious. I know that it was His hand that brought us together, and it was Him that allowed such a depth between us. He gave us the gift of this friendship."

Eric paused, searching my face for a sign of agreement. *He's trying to say as many nice things as possible so he can let me down easy,* I mentally cringed as I gave him a little nod to continue. He took another deep breath and charged ahead. "Well, lately I've really been struggling with this whole thing because . . . well, because I'd never met a girl I could imagine spending the rest of my life with . . . until . . . uh, until you."

He looked down, careful not to meet my gaze as he reached out to straighten an upside down ladybug with his pointer finger.

I was speechless. After weeks of convincing myself he could never want someone like me, after hours of agonizing over the fact that he would never see me as the kind of woman he would want to marry . . . his words were like a sudden, unexpected yet glorious sunrise to my soul.

I swallowed hard to contain the rising emotion. My hands began to shake with adrenaline.

"You see, even though you were my best friend and I was also really attracted to you. . . ." Eric paused, his eyes scanning the bike path below us. "This may sound strange, Les," he continued, shifting uncomfortably on the grass. "But I made a decision a long time ago never to begin another relationship with a girl until I knew it was my wife."

Spellbound, I nodded, remembering all the times he had spoken about wanting to save himself completely for the woman he would one day marry, remembering how I had envied her, whoever she was.

Nervously, I chewed on my lower lip and waited with baited breath for the words that would follow.

"Well, that's why I haven't said anything to you about moving beyond a friendship, even though I wanted to," he went on softly. "But these past few weeks as I've prayed about all this. . . ." his voice broke suddenly and he looked away.

My eyes stayed glued to his face, blood pounding in my ears. Paralyzed with shock, the reality of where this conversation was leading left me feeling as though I were watching myself in a dream. Inwardly, I longed for him to hurry and finish the thought he was struggling so hard to express.

He took another deep breath and finally said, "Les, I really feel that God has made it clear to me that someday we'll be together." He looked up at me, finally able to meet my gaze as he went on. "Maybe not right away, but I feel God has shown me that He is preparing me . . . to one day be . . . your husband."

My breath caught in my throat as I drank in the words he had just uttered and the sincerity written across his tender face.

He studied my expression and ventured delicately, "The only reason I felt comfortable telling you this is because, well, I've been talking this over with your dad. He told me that both he and your mom felt you would be ready to hear me say those words." He hesitated, then added quietly, "They thought you would feel the same way toward me."

I gazed back at him for several long seconds, trembling even more violently as the moment finally began to sink in.

Eric cares about me as more than a friend! He feels God is knitting our lives together, preparing us for marriage . . . to each other!

A thrill went through my entire body. Unspeakable joy began to warm me from head to toe. Tears of utter relief and happiness began to flow freely down my face as I stared at the man I knew I would one day call my husband.

"Leslie?" he questioned hesitantly, his eyes beckoning me to speak. "Do you, . . . I mean, do you feel the same way?"

Rousing myself from my state of numbness and shock, I finally found my voice.

A radiant smile of delight creased my face and I uttered a single word that seemed as if it made the Heavens stand and cheer. "Yes," I stated softly.

And it was in that unforgettable instant I felt tender arms around me. Not the arms of Eric, but of my gentle Lord Jesus. He was smiling at my childlike heart, full of wonder and delight, full of innocence once again, as if it had never been stolen away from me. And He was softly whispering words to my heart I would never forget . . . *My precious child, you cannot even imagine how beautiful dreams can be . . . when I make them come true.*

The Ludy Kitchen
August 28, 1992

-leslie-

barb, are you ready for me to fire up the grill?" Win strolled into the kitchen wearing a bright green "Number One Dad" apron and holding a huge bottle of barbecue sauce.

Barb was too busy searching the cabinet for a serving tray to hear him.

"Before you do that, Daddy, could you help me open this jar of pickles for the potato salad?" Krissy sweetly questioned.

"Has anyone seen my red soccer sweatshirt?" Mark bellowed, frantically searching the room as if the missing article of clothing might be hiding under a dinner plate or casserole dish.

"Hey! It's not *your* red soccer sweatshirt—it's mine!" Eric argued loudly from his station at the kitchen sink, where he had been assigned to rinse and chop tomatoes and onions for the condiment tray.

"Mary! Get down from there!" Barb scolded, having just discovered the overweight and aging family cat positioned smugly on the countertop, eyeing the banana cream pie.

I tried to stifle a smile as I observed the typical chaos of a pre-meal experience at the Ludy home. As I turned back to filling tall glasses with iced tea, I suddenly sneezed.

"Mark, take Mary outside," Win requested as he struggled with an impossibly tight jar of pickles. "Leslie is allergic to her and so is Rich. The rest of the Runkles are going to be here any minute."

"Come on, Mare," Mark cooed in the soupy voice he always used when addressing animals or babies—a mix between Elmo after breathing helium and Miss Piggy with laryngitis. He scooped up the wildly protesting cat and headed for the back door.

"Hello?" I heard my mom's voice question from the front hall.

"They're here!" Krissy rang excitedly, adding another blob of mayonnaise to her potato salad masterpiece.

"Come on innnn!" Barb's soprano vibrated throughout the house.

Eric leaned close to my ear. "You ready for tonight, Les?" he whispered with concern on his face.

I noticed my hands were shaking as I poured from the tall pitcher. Was it really only yesterday we had sat on the grassy hill and had that memorable conversation? It already seemed like weeks had passed. I had walked around in a happy daze since the moment he had unveiled his heart. As we had continued to talk about our new relationship, we had both decided it was important to share what had happened with our two families. As much as I loved and trusted all the members of the Runkles and Ludy clan, I was nervous. I knew my parents had given their wholehearted stamp of approval upon what God was doing, and I suspected Eric's family felt the same way. But the thought of publicly talking about all that had been happening between Eric and me still left me feeling awkward. *Lord, please guide and direct the conversation this evening,* I prayed internally. A subtle peace began to flow over my heart. I gave Eric a shaky smile. "I think I'm ready," I replied to his unanswered question. "It's just going to be weird."

"Do you still feel it's time to let our families know what's going on?" he asked seriously.

I took a deep breath. "Yes," I finally answered. "I know it's important to invite them into this whole thing. It's just, . . ." my voice trailed off as the kitchen grew quiet. Win had exited to the back porch to work magic on the raw hamburger patties as Mark struggled with an indignant Mary near the screen door. Krissy was intently focused on the celery chopping that she was diligently engaged in, and Barb was humming softly as she rummaged in the refrigerator. In the distance, I could hear shuffling from the entryway as my family removed their shoes and began moving toward the kitchen.

Eric followed my uncomfortable gaze around the room and took my elbow, leading me into a private corner of the hall.

"Okay," he encouraged, his voice low. "Go on with what you were saying."

"Well," I continued in a hushed whisper. "I just never thought my family would be this involved in . . . you know, this area of my life." I sighed in reflection. "I mean, this will probably be uncomfortable at first. But I really feel God has an important reason for both our families being a part of this from the very beginning."

Eric nodded his agreement. "I really want to honor our parents as we move forward," he added with conviction. "I'm not fully sure how to do that yet, but I want to try my best."

As we moved slowly back toward the kitchen Eric muttered ruefully over his shoulder, "I just hope my brother stays under control tonight! His favorite pastime is embarrassing me, and this would be the perfect opportunity!"

———

a half-hour later, when the burgers had been expertly grilled by the Ludy family chef, the potato salad had been reverently placed on the table by Krissy, and Mark had located Eric's red sweatshirt and wrenched it over his faded Denver Broncos t-shirt, the two families took their seats around the Ludy dining room table.

"Join our family circle," Win invited, right on cue as we all joined hands.

After a short but eloquent prayer offered by my dad, a bustle of activity once again surrounded the room as food was passed, catsup and mustard were retrieved from the refrigerator, and Mary the cat howled loudly from her place of exile on the back porch.

Once all plates had been filled and all ten of us were contentedly savoring the delicious meal, Barb spoke up.

"Well, I'm curious!" she said mischievously. "I'm ready to hear what's going on between these two!" Her eyes danced eagerly to the other end of the table, where Eric was kindly offering me a second helping of potato salad.

Everyone turned to gaze at us and I could feel my face starting to flush. Eric reached for his glass of tea and began awkwardly swirling the ice cubes back and forth. After stretching the expectant silence out for as long as possible, he looked around the table and took a deep breath.

"Well," he began slowly. "Les and I have been doing a lot of praying about our friendship over the past few weeks. I've been really feeling for a while now that I wanted there to be more than just a friendship between us." Eric paused to scowl impatiently at his brother, who was peering over Krissy's shoulder with a delighted Cheshire cat grin.

"Anyway," Eric continued, attempting to ignore Mark's smirking face, "I didn't want to say anything to Leslie because I wanted to know for sure that God was behind it before I took the next step."

Win nodded pleasantly to encourage Eric to continue.

"I met with Rich and he confirmed that he really felt this friendship was from God. He also said something that day that really took me off guard. He gave me his blessing to pursue a relationship with Leslie in any way God might lead me."

I looked curiously at my dad, who just smiled calmly in return.

"I wasn't even thinking about a relationship with Leslie at that point," Eric went on. "I mean, she's five years younger than me! But I kept praying about everything. And pretty soon, looking back over our friendship, I just saw God's fingerprints all over it."

Eric's eyes rested briefly on my mom's intent face. "Janet," he asked, "do you remember that night back in February when we were over at your house for dinner? You came up to me after the prayer time and you told me you felt that God wanted me to know that what was spoken to me that night was from Him."

My mom nodded as the memory returned.

"Well," Eric stated carefully, "I had been struggling all night with a thought that kept floating through my head that Leslie was going to one day be my wife. And I kept thinking it was Satan trying to distract me. I never thought it might be *God* speaking to my heart! And even that night after you spoke those words to me, Janet, I didn't think it meant anything. But a few weeks ago when I was praying about my friendship with Leslie, I was reminded of that night and I realized it had been God speaking to me all along!"

My mom's eyebrows lifted in surprise and she gave a little chuckle. "Wow!" she stated. "If I had known what was going on in your head the whole time. . . ." Soft laughter filled the room as we all followed her meaning.

"There were hundreds of little confirmations like that as I looked back over the past eight months," Eric was saying. "And for the first time, it was like scales fell off my eyes, and I could see so clearly that Leslie . . ." he paused dramatically as our family members leaned forward expectantly. "*Leslie* was the one I'd been praying for all these years."

An emotion-packed moment of silence enveloped the room as each person silently took in the words just spoken. I ventured a glance around the table. Krissy's eyes were shining with joy. Barb was beaming, staring reflectively at the white tablecloth. My mom had taken my dad's hand and was smiling tenderly. Win had folded his hands in front of him and was nodding slowly in approval. Both of my brothers were staring at each other with expressions of great surprise. And Mark was still smirking triumphantly at Eric.

"So, when's the wedding?" Mark blurted, breaking through the quiet with all the delicacy of a speeding freight train.

Eric gave his brother a warning look, "We're not engaged or anything, Marky," he said pointedly. "We just feel God is preparing us for a future together, and we feel it's time to take our friendship to the next level."

Eric cleared his throat to signify that he wanted to make an additional point. Expectant silence filled the room as we waited for him to speak. "If you all don't mind," he began awkwardly, "we would really like to keep this relationship just between the two families for a while and a few close friends. This is all so new to us and we want to hear God's voice as we move forward. We don't want to be distracted by other people's input, other than those few we feel have true wisdom to offer us." He paused and let his eyes roam to each face present. "Does that make sense?" he finished uncertainly. Each family member nodded thoughtfully to let him know they understood.

"Well, I'm excited!" Win proclaimed from his place at the head of the table. "It's so neat to see how God has been there every step of the way!" Sounds of agreement filled the air as he added, "And I would love it if we could all go around the table and share our own perspectives about how we've seen God put this relationship together."

I will never forget the hour that followed. I sat stunned in complete amazement as each member of Eric's family, and each member of my own family spoke about how God had shown them individually that this relationship was truly of Him. They exhorted us, encouraged us, and prayed for us. Even my brothers, who had basically been in the dark that anything was going on, were excited and supportive. I was filled with the awesome realization that Eric and I were not alone in our newfound relationship. We had eight people who loved us who were totally committed to being our teammates in whatever the future might hold.

As the unforgettable evening drew to a close and the Ludy-Runkle clan sat around sipping coffee or nibbling the remainder of the banana cream pie, my dad spoke.

"I believe that God is doing something here that goes beyond just Eric and Leslie," he said in his usual calm way. "I believe God wants to use this relationship to affect the world. Through the example of their testimony, I believe God wants to restore to their generation the kind of purity and commitment He intended in relationships." My dad looked at Eric and me, a solemn challenge in his caring blue eyes.

"The enemy will no doubt try to come against you and distract you from the path God has set before you," he said quietly. "But if you keep God at the center of your relationship as you have done thus far, I believe you have the potential to do this one hundred percent the right way . . . God's way!"

Leslie's Bedroom
September 2, 1992

i slowly made my way up the staircase and opened my bedroom door, trying to mentally soothe the heaviness in my heart. I knew it was time for Eric to leave, but it was hard to believe that I wouldn't see his eager brown eyes or ever-ready smile for five long months. I brushed a tear away and snatched my pink satiny pillow from my bed, hugging it tightly against my chest as I approached the window and looked down into the street where Eric was waiting for a sign of me.

As I stood looking out at him, he grinned bravely, letting his gaze linger on my tormented face a moment before waving slowly and opening the door of the red Toyota Camry.

Within moments, the engine started and with one last look that spoke volumes and yet another wave of his hand, he was gone. With him, he took a piece of my heart.

I took a deep, shaky breath and felt the fatigue from the emotionally charged night. My mind drifted back to the conversation I'd had with Eric a few short hours ago. We had been walking together along the bike path behind my house, preparing for our final goodbye.

"It may be a while before it's even time to start thinking seriously about engagement and marriage," Eric had said as a warm breeze toyed with his hair. "So I think it's important for us to stay focused on the friendship aspect of our relationship." He stopped walking and turned to face me. "There are so many times when I want to reach out and just hold you, Les." His voice grew quiet with feeling.

"And there are words that I desperately want to say to you." He reached up and softly touched my cheek for a fraction of a second, then withdrew his hand. "But I want to be careful. Even though I believe God is preparing us to be married someday, I really feel we need to give our emotions for each other to Him. I don't want this relationship to be built on our own emotional feelings. I want it to be centered around God."

I chewed on my lower lip, knowing that he was right. I, too, had felt a caution in my own heart not to rush headlong into a passionate romance just because we felt that God was putting our relationship together. Both of us had been in past relationships we'd built ourselves, and experienced the disasterous outcome firsthand. With everything in me I longed for this relationship with Eric to be different, to be built by God from start to finish. I knew how easy it would be for me to get in the way.

"I agree with you," I told him sincerely. "I know that I have a lot of growing up and maturing to do before I'll be ready for marriage. And in the meantime, I really feel we need to entrust our emotions to God, just like you said. I know He'll show us when the time is right to take this relationship to the next level."

Now, standing in front of my bedroom window as the Camry turned down Rambling Rose Road and disappeared, I still knew it had been the right decision. Yet a disappointed ache filled my heart. A goodbye to the man who held my heart—without even one kiss or a tender 'I love you'—seemed so empty. I knew it was too soon for that kind of physical affection or those kind of strong words, and yet . . .

My eye suddenly caught sight of a beautifully wrapped package on my dresser. With a gasp I rushed over to it. Examining the purple and white wrapping paper, I noticed a tiny hand-written message, "For my girl."

Tears flowed freely as I cautiously opened the lovely paper. Inside was a framed drawing of Eric smiling at me in his unique Eric-Ludy way. The picture was obviously the master artwork of his brother Mark. My heart swelled as I carefully placed the treasure on my dresser. Shaking the package gently, I realized that there was more. Reaching inside, my fingers curled around a small, square-shaped box. I withdrew my hand, holding tightly to the additional gift. It was a tape. On the cover was a drawing of the two of us, sitting side by side on the same grassy hill where we had the first conversation about our future together.

Almost in a daze, I put the tape in my stereo unit and turned up the volume. A soft and beautiful melody flooded the room and I sank down on my bed in awe. He had written me a song!

As his voice belted out the unforgettable tune, tears of joy streamed down my cheeks.

You knew exactly what I needed, Lord! I whispered in amazement. You are so faithful! You knew I needed a romantic gift like this to have peace about Eric leaving. Oh Lord, thank You for this! I feel like a princess.

I listened to the song at least five times before I finally drifted off to sleep, my heart at rest, knowing that God was holding this new romance in the palm of His hand. If I obeyed even when it didn't make sense, He would never let me down.

My Girl Leslie
Written by Eric Ludy

Do I yet know you, do you yet know me
There are so many treasures still to find
Like a diamond in the rough, the chipping away is tough
But what we find within is ever priceless

I think I've seen a glimpse of eternity
When I look upon what He's placed between us
We've only just begun to taste and feel His kingdom
Skipping through the meadows up in Heaven

I sort of know you, you know me kinda too
What really is there left to find
I feel that God is saying, "My children, you can't imagine
The journey I've set ahead of you"

It's a journey to discover the pure and perfect lover,
Centered upon God and not one another
If I don't yet fully know you
I believe I'm starting to
Witness a flower bloom before me
In my girl . . . Leslie

The Secret

-eric-

keeping a secret for two years is fairly easy when it is something trivial like having a snowball stowed away in your freezer. But when it involves something more central like having a girl stowed away in your heart, it's a little more challenging to hide.

Marky of course knew all about my budding relationship with Leslie, but was sworn to silence. And I'm sure he thoroughly enjoyed seeing me attempt to keep it a secret from everyone else at Twin Oaks Ranch.

"So Eric? Do you have a love in your life?"

"Uh, . . . I have Jesus!" I would creatively counter and bolster my spiritual status at the same time.

"Eric, who are you always sneaking off and talking to on the phone?"

"Uh, . . . what do you mean sneaking off?" I would innocently mumble. "I'm just looking for a little privacy in which to talk to friends and family back home!"

"Who's this Leslie Runkles?" The mail lady would inquire. "She sure is providing you with a lot of reading material this semester!"

"Uh, . . . yeah, she's a sweet girl. A good friend of Marky's and mine from Colorado."

As the weeks, the months, and the years passed, our secret remained secure. There were those with their hunches, but even the most observant Sherlock Holmes among them wouldn't have known the true depth and beauty of what was taking place between the two of us. There were moments when we were tested, but creative verbal maneuvering always provided a slick way out.

I always referred to Leslie as my "very good friend" from Colorado.

When Melinda from Bible study tried to fix me up with her niece, I graciously declined under the pretext of "not being interested." Over a seven month period, Chuck from college asked me to accompany his "available" sister and him to a concert in the park, a miniature golf course, a Bronco's game, a greyhound race, a movie, and an amusement park. I was strangely "unavailable" each and every time he asked.

"She's a very good friend," I animatedly squawked.

"Well, I have a lot of good friends, Eric," my nosey buddy Ryan reasoned, "but none of them send me dozens of freshly baked homemade cookies in a large box with hearts scribbled on it."

"It was sent to Marky, too!" I argued. "Look! It says, 'AND Mark Ludy.'"

"Yeah," Ryan continued like a pesky fly, "but *your* name is written first and in big bubble letters. His is written as if it were a passing thought to cover the tracks of your secret little love affair."

There are two kinds of secrets: there are those that hide deceit and crooked ways, and there are those that hide buried treasure and amazing surprises. Les and I were often-times bent over laughing after some of our run-ins with the probing Ryans of the world. We knew we weren't covering up some political scandal or some juicy piece of sexual devilishness. We were secretly treasuring an intimate knowledge that became sweeter and more valuable as time passed. We were holding on to a great surprise that in due time would give rise to many "I knew it! I knew it all along!" responses. But Leslie and I were certain that no one could possibly know the depth of what we were experiencing in our blossoming love story . . . not even us.

The Phone Calls

—leslie—

i eagerly snatched the blue phone out of its cradle on the first ring.

"Hello?" I asked a little too breathlessly, reaching out to close my bedroom door with my foot.

"Hey!" came the familiar voice that never failed to make my heart leap with excitement.

"Hi!" I nervously unwound the hopelessly tangled phone cord as I waited for him to get the conversation going.

"How're ya' doing?" his voice was full of tender concern.

"Good! How's it going there?"

"Well, God's really using this time to stretch me, Les. There are parts of this trip to New Orleans that have been really difficult. I mean, I'm staying in a homeless shelter trying to serve people who pretty much hate me! But He's been faithful each step of the way. I have some amazing stories to share with you! But first, tell me what's been going on in your life lately? What has God been up to?"

I sighed in reflection, trying to verbally capture all the many things that had been happening in my heart and mind lately.

"Um, well, it's hard to summarize. I guess I really see how God is using this time to prepare me for the future," I began. "I think that probably the most significant thing happening right now is what God is teaching me through the books I've been reading."

"What kind of books?" Eric's enthusiasm for what God was doing in my life was evident even from over 1,000 miles away.

"Biographies, mostly, like the stories of Corrie Ten Boom and Jim Elliot."

For nearly a half-hour, Eric listened intently—interjecting questions every so often—to my narration of what I had learned from studying the lives of these great Christians. My heart filled with the warmth and deep appreciation I felt each time I had the rare treat of a long phone conversation with Eric. Being a traveling missionary, he didn't have many opportunities to call, but whenever he did, I savored every moment like a child lingers over a lollipop.

Sometimes it amazed me that our being so far away from each other for so long wasn't more difficult. But truthfully, though it was certainly not an easy way to build a relationship, I could see God's gentle hand of wisdom in our separation. Instead of giving into the temptation to build my life around Eric, I was able to continue building my life around the Lord Jesus Christ. I was in the crucial years of my development as an individual, and while I was secure in my relationship with Eric, I wasn't distracted by having him around every day.

The decision we had made to focus mainly on the friendship aspect of our relationship, and to entrust our emotions to God during this "in-between" time, had proven to be a very wise choice. Though Eric and I deeply cherished each other's companionship and treasured each letter and phone call, the focus of our communication was mostly on what God was doing in each other's lives. We didn't want to awaken the strong, romantic emotional floodgates too soon. I knew the passion would come when we both knew the time was right. In the meantime I was so thankful for the spiritual unity God was strengthening between us.

eric and I moved on to talk about his venture to minister at a homeless shelter in inner city New Orleans. I was fascinated and inspired by his tireless pursuit of God and the way he saw each situation as nothing short of one exciting challenge after the next.

"Uh, Les?" Eric's voice had lowered substantially and I put my hand over my free ear to hear him better. "I really want to keep talking, but uh, I'm on a pay phone in kind of a rough part of town . . . and I think . . . well, a drug deal is taking place a few feet away from me, so I'd better, uh, I'd better get outa' here!"

As I replaced the phone into its cradle that night, I closed my eyes tightly and uttered a prayer for Eric's safety. A rueful smile crept over my face as I once again realized . . . *life with Eric Ludy will be one big adventure!* And by now I knew I didn't want it any other way.

Painful Goodbyes

-leslie-

Saying goodbye to someone you care about deeply is like ripping a scab off a wound; it takes a while for the pain to stop smarting, and even longer for the scar to finally heal. I have often wondered why God chose to breathe life into my relationship with Eric while I was still so young—years away from being ready for marriage. Because as time went by, the goodbyes piled up, one on top of the other like a collection of fall leaves cascading down from a shedding tree.

After the missionary school had ended in February, Eric continued his travels, pursuing various ministry ventures. He had a vast array of opportunities to choose from—none of which were located where I was—Colorado.

It's not that it was easy for him to say goodbye to me each time, going off to reach his world with the Gospel. But we both knew that I was still growing up. And it just wasn't time for the next step in our relationship. While I finished high school and attended to all the other aspects of my young, maturing life, I knew it was important for Eric to pursue the callings God had placed before him.

He had come home to rest for a few short weeks the summer of 1993, and the time spent with him had been like a warm refreshing breeze to my spirit. One afternoon we were sitting together in the Ludy family living room. By the look in his eyes, I could tell another goodbye was shortly on the horizon.

So, Les, it's a really great opportunity, but I just need to know how you feel about it," Eric studied me earnestly. "Do you think I should go to Michigan to teach for a year?"

I ran my hand distractedly along the soft fabric of the Ludys' flowered sofa as I thought of a way to reply. Another goodbye, another tearing out of a piece of my heart and taking it with him . . . Yet, God had always been faithful to provide the grace I needed to make it through the times of separation. I knew that no matter how much a part of my future he might be, I could not build my life around Eric Ludy. I needed to build it around Jesus Christ.

"I think you should go," I told him with conviction in my voice. "I feel it's what God has called you to do."

"You do?" he replied, watching my face carefully. "I mean, Les, it would mean that I would be away for another whole year. Are you . . . are you sure?"

"Yes," I said firmly, nodding my certainty. "I mean, I will really miss you. But . . . it's just not time for, you know . . ."

"The next step," he finished for me, nodding quietly in agreement.

"You know, Les," Eric said, picking at the leather band on his watch, "no matter how far apart we are, it's God who holds this relationship together. I so appreciate that you can allow me to follow where I feel He is leading me. I know that God will show us when it's time to move things to the next step in our relationship." He looked at me with a hint of tears glistening in his eyes, "And I hope it's soon. Because I'm really going to miss you . . . again!"

━

So once again on a warm August evening, I found myself standing on my front porch, waving slowly as the red Toyota

Camry made its way down the street, turning off Rambling Rose Road and headed 1,200 miles away to Kalamazoo, Michigan. Brushing tears from my eyes, I turned to re-enter the house, a silent prayer in my heart.

Lord, give me grace for this year. You have always been faithful in my relationship with Eric, and I know that even if we must be separated for ten more years, you will give me grace for each and every day. Help me trust You.

Goodbyes are often unspeakably painful. And yet, with each goodbye we utter comes the fresh promise of the beginning of a brand new season of our life. And with each season, there is a new life lesson to be learned from our Maker. Every goodbye Eric and I spoke inevitably drew us closer together in the end. And with each mile of separation from Eric, my Lord drew all the nearer to my vulnerable heart.

The Letters

Eric,

I feel like when you arrive from Michigan in March you won't recognize me. I'm changing. Deep down inside God is shaping me and molding me into a woman that fears and loves Him. I am coming to understand, in a whole new light, how tender and gentle my Father in heaven is. I'm seeing my terrible selfishness and I find myself crying out to God to make me more selfless and servant hearted.

It is so obvious to me why God has me single and alone right now. He wants me to learn how to be fulfilled and whole in Him, because only then would I be ready to share my life with someone else. I know that this time of loneliness for me is preparing me for leadership in the years ahead. I know that this painful realization of my sinfulness is teaching me about my need for Jesus Christ all the more.

I miss you so much. But I'm glad you're not here. Because, even though the Spirit's probing and conviction in my life is grievous and exacting, I know it's shaping me into the woman He has called me to become.

In Christ's love,

Les

a letter represents something far more than a kiss ever could. It evidences thoughtfulness and the gift of time. While a kiss can prove tender, it must overcome the stigma of impulsiveness to truly display love. A letter on the other hand, when written in the spirit of ardor and romance—even if it never mentions passion—strokes the heart deeper than any other form of physical touch. A kiss cannot be felt again and again from great distance, but a letter can be read and reread thousands of times. A kiss only familiarizes lips with the physical body of a lover. A letter familiarizes the heart, mind, and soul. Maybe that's why God chose to write us a letter.

My girl,

I'm lonely too. I often feel like I'm the only one alive who sees God's tears. I ache as I think of those Christians suffering for Christ around the world. Yesterday I finished a book about the persecuted church in Romania. I don't know what to do practically in response. But I know that if I don't feel pain and sorrow, something is seriously wrong with me.

Les, I want to give my life for Jesus. If I'm going to die, I want to die a heroic death for Him. I want others to see in my life the hope, the peace, and the joy that can only be found in our precious Christ.

Every day it seems God has a gem of truth hidden for me to discover. I want to live expectantly, knowing that the God of the entire universe is intimately sharing every moment of every day with me. If we lived in accordance with that reality day in and day out, we would be different people, wouldn't we?

I miss being able to see your sweet face. Please remember that you are the treasure of my heart!

Your boy,

Eric

Preparation

time flew by. While Eric kept an amazingly active schedule teaching in Michigan, I held down a calendar as busy as most high school seniors. But my life was completely different than the usual American teenager. Ever since I made the decision to leave public high school, finish my education at home, and put Jesus Christ first, I decided that I wanted my life to revolve around things that truly mattered. I was no longer consumed by the endless cycle of meaningless activities that had once filled my days. Every now and then I would think back to that time not so very long ago, when I had thought I had everything a young girl could want—yet was miserable and empty inside. I remembered that time in my life only as one remembers a dream. I was now such a completely different person.

I realized that what now occupied my time was preparation. I had no idea what the future held for me, but as I prayed about my life I felt sure that God was using this year to ready me for what was coming.

I am busy, I had written to Eric in a recent letter, *but my life is so full of rich meaning. I know God is preparing me in every way— spiritually, emotionally, and physically—for the future. I spend hours alone with Him each day, studying His word, reading accounts of heroes of the faith. This time with Him is my sustenance. And I know I am learning and growing in my walk with God more than ever before. This time is so priceless.*

Studying music, leading worship, helping with community outreaches, encouraging young girls in their faith, and allowing myself to be mentored by godly older women were just a few of the items on my weekly agenda. I had even started getting opportunities to share my testimony at local churches, women's Bible studies, and youth groups.

My life was indeed full. I was growing and maturing rapidly. But as the year progressed, the subtle void in my heart began to speak louder and louder. I was missing Eric. As the early signs of spring began to show, I began to long to have him near, a longing more intense than I'd ever felt before.

"Is it time, Lord, for the next step in my relationship with Eric?" I would pray earnestly every night, but receiving no answer, would drift to sleep, asking for the grace to make it through another day without him.

When I talked to Eric on the phone, I could hear excitement and passion for his life and work on the other side of the country. I knew he missed me, but he gave no indication that he was growing as restless as I.

One evening I took a walk at dusk. My eyes rested on the brilliant sunset painting the horizon over the glorious Rockies. I thought about all God had done in my life over the past few years. He had never failed me.

a crisp breeze rustled around me and I zipped up my fleece jacket against the chill. Finding a secluded rock to sit on, I reached inside the small backpack I had brought along on my walk and withdrew a leather journal and pen. Opening to a fresh sheet, my hand began to flow over the paper, pouring out my thoughts and fears.

Graduation is looming closer and closer, I hastily scrawled, *and I still have no idea what I'm going to do this next summer or fall. My* dad has been encouraging me to pursue college and to major in music. And just yesterday my mom gave me a brochure about helping with orphanages in Russia for a year. The pen lifted from the journal as I paused and looked into the sky, searching for expression for the emotions swirling ruthlessly in my soul. Taking a deep breath, I resumed the fluid motion of writing. *But I can't seem to make a decision. Deep down, I think the real reason I can't decide what to do is because I miss Eric so much. Life seems empty without him. Lord, help me be patient. Help me wait for your perfect timing. When it's the right time for him to propose to me, I know you'll show him. Help me trust You.*

Suddenly an unexplained shiver of excitement shot through me. As I gazed at the beautiful mountain scene in front of me I couldn't seem to shake the feeling that something amazing was about to take place in my life . . . and very soon.

Spring Break
March 1994

—eric—

What is it?" I excitedly rang.

"I'm not going to tell you what's inside!" Leslie playfully joked. "Why do you think I wrapped it up and put a bow on it? It's supposed to be a surprise!"

Leslie knew I loved surprises. In a matter of seconds I had removed the blue pinstriped paper and the satiny white bow.

"It's for all the letters I've sent you." She clarified as I cheerfully scrutinized my newfound gift.

"You see," she continued while grabbing the gift out of my hands and snuggling up beside me on the couch, "this one is for you. It says 'letters from Les.' And this one is for me."

"Ah, 'letters from Eric!'" I enthusiastically applauded as I cherished the cuteness of my friend and her adorable and thoughtful gift.

"You've been saving all my letters, haven't you?" She interrogated with a burst of sudden suspicion.

"Of course I have!" I countered. "They are my most prized and valuable possessions!"

She smiled, looked down at the floor, blushed, and shrugged her right shoulder as if to say, *I like it when you say things like that!*

"See?" she said. "I've been keeping everything *you* send me."

With that she whipped open the "letters from Eric" to reveal a multitudinous stack of letters all signed by Eric Ludy.

"Which one is your favorite?" I inquired.

"Whichever one is longest!" She playfully responded.

"What about that three line poem I wrote you?" I pleaded.

"It was nice, it just wasn't long enough!" she spoke with a twinkle in her emerald eyes.

"Okay, my next letter will be over ten pages, then." I shot back. "But you have to write me a long one too!"

"But not too long," she chided. "If I write too many ten-pagers, you'll run out of room in the notebook I made for you!"

～

Our letters were our kisses. They rarely talked about passionate things, but they were romantic. It was a unique sort of romance though. It was a love that started upside down as contrasted with the relationships of our age, beginning first with the intimate touch of a heart rather than the intimate touch of the physical body.

"Can you believe it's been nearly two-and-a-half years since we first met?" I pondered as we sat in the rickety swing behind the Runkles' house.

"Sometimes it seems a lot longer than that," Leslie added.

We sat in the moonlight, silently pondering what God had done between us.

"Did you like your gift?" Leslie meekly inquired.

"I loved it!" I beamed.

"When you drove up to the house today," Leslie softly whispered, "I thought I was going to explode with excitement. I've missed you, Eric."

"Les?" I carefully ventured, "I have so much I want to say to you. There are words I desperately want to speak to you, but . . ." my voice trailed off.

Leslie tenderly looked up into my eyes and subtly shifted her body on the swing to better listen and understand.

"I'm feeling things Les, that I've never before felt. Deeper things, deeper emotions, deeper desires."

Leslie nodded and bit her bottom lip.

"Up to this moment I felt like I could return to Michigan and continue to wait. But something so pure, so strong, so passionate is opening up within my heart. I really want to be with you. I want to be close to you. I want to touch you. . ." Then with a smile and a turning of my eyes toward the ground I said, "Les, I want to . . . kiss you!"

Both of us awkwardly looked somewhere other than into each other's eyes. The moment was strange, yet mythically beautiful. It was full of enchantment, tenderness, and truth. Both of us were experiencing something overwhelmingly powerful—the wave of emotional love.

"I already feel like my five days here are coming to an end . . . and I just arrived three hours ago! Les, I'm tired of saying goodbye. I'm tired of not being able to tell you what I'm feeling for you deep down inside my soul. Les, I know God smiles on patience, but patience sure doesn't smile on me. It hurts. It tortures me."

I paused and looked at her, studied her in the moonlight. She was unable to return my gaze as her eyes carefully examined the roseate nail polish on her right pinky finger.

"I desperately hope it's not much longer!" I moaned. "But I know it's going to be worth the pain."

Leslie finally raised her eyes to mine.

"When it's time Les, I'll come like a knight to sweep you off your feet!"

g oodbye!" I whispered through the open window of my car. "I'll be back as soon as I possibly can!"

"Like a knight," Leslie added, "to sweep your princess off her feet?"

"It'll be better than the fairy tales!" I declared as I put the car into gear and began moseying down Rambling Rose Road.

The tears I saw in her eyes as I turned to begin the long journey to Michigan were too much for my manly soul. As I sped down the familiar road I found myself sobbing with the pain of leaving her. She was the most beautiful, most sweet, most treasured jewel in my life . . . and I was driving away.

No longer was our relationship a secret. The night before, we had shared the amazing details of our unfolding love story with a gathering of sixty of our closest friends. There were cheers, tears, and many hugs passed around. As exciting as it was to finally share it, the pain that accompanied the awareness that we would once again be over a thousand miles apart was unbearable and unforgiving in its weight.

No longer was this just a friendship. Our hearts were now warmed with something far greater than mutual respect, kindred sympathies, and tender admiration. We were experiencing love, unmitigated and unleashed. We were mesmerized by attractions toward each other that burned within us like hot coals in a campfire.

Lord, I prayed while tears dripped off my chin and moistened the front of my sweatshirt, *please let it be soon. Please don't let me jump ahead of You. But please, please, let it be soon.*

Allegan, Michigan

April 1994

—eric—

expectation is the main ingredient in the recipe for abiding joy. For months I had been praying for one very specific item. For months I had been expectant, and for months absolutely nothing had happened to even hint that God was paying attention.

"That's what George Mueller did," Krissy reminded me.

"What do you mean?" I asked my sister, who for the past school year had also functioned as my housemate in a quaint little home just outside the quaint town of Allegan, a tiny village near the city of Kalamazoo, where we both taught.

"He didn't tell people of his needs," she noted, "he only told God. And God always supernaturally provided!"

And that is exactly what we decided to do. Every morning and night Krissy and I knelt on the brownish carpeting of our charming little homestead and asked God to somehow, someway provide me with an engagement ring to give to Leslie.

"Eric!" Krissy exhorted as the weeks and months passed and nothing happened. "God loves it when we take even the little things to Him. Keep trusting and He will bless you!"

---

the moment my eyes opened that April morning I had a surge of anticipation. At 5:03 A.M., I lumbered down the creaky hallway towards the bathroom. A winsome smile danced across my face like one of those ballerinas in the Nutcracker. I noticed light emanating from under Krissy's door as I stumbled into the darkened bathroom.

As I showered and dressed, preparing myself for another day of teaching, a bubbling expectancy flitted through my mind causing a little chuckle to play off my vocal chords. Finally, while combing my hair, I just couldn't hold it in any longer.

"Krissy!" I yelled, momentarily turning my attention from my brown curls. "Krissy!"

After about twenty seconds, Krissy burst out her bedroom door and popped her head into the bathroom. "What? What? What is it?" She anxiously shouted.

"Nothing." I said calmly. Then matter-of-factly and with a twinkle in my eye I said, "I'm just excited."

Krissy's face grew mildly disdainful and she rolled her eyes. "That's wonderful, Eric!" she stammered with a slight hint of sarcasm in her voice. With that she turned and ventured back into her bedroom to conclude her rudely interrupted quiet time.

After I finished with my curls I searched around the countertop for my facial lotion. It was nowhere to be seen. *Oh,* I remembered, *I left it in my coat pocket.*

Energetically I danced down the creaky hallway towards the front room to reclaim my misplaced lotion. When I found my red coat and reached into its oversized pockets I found something in addition to my lotion—an envelope.

The envelope said "for Eric Ludy" on the outside. Immediately I knew what it was. Every couple of weeks, one of the cute little girls I taught would color in a coloring book page, rip it out, stick it in an envelope, and scrawl something similar to "for Eric" on the outside. *How cute,* I thought. Then grabbing my all-important lotion I raced back to the bathroom to finish getting ready.

Curiosity got the better of me when I arrived back in front of the bathroom mirror. I had to know which kindergartner had been so thoughtful to draw me a picture, so I opened up the envelope.

I carefully removed a piece of notebook paper and noticed that it contained something completely different than what I had been expecting. Studiously I unwrapped the college-ruled piece of writing paper and inside . . . I found . . . a pile of . . . *money.*

I delicately placed the pile on the counter as if it were incriminating evidence at a murder scene, then looking into the mirror I shouted, "Krissy! Krissy!"

I heard shifting and banging in the adjacent room. Krissy made her way through her door and reluctantly into the bathroom. "What?" she stated with growing frustration.

Staring at her knitted eyebrows through the mirror, I pointed at the contents of the envelope that lingered near the far eastern edge of the formica counter. "Ayawahua" I mumbled attempting to speak.

Krissy's eyes burst open and she approached the envelope's hallowed contents. She took one glance up at me as if to say, "How exciting!"

She carefully picked up the stack of bills and began to count out loud. In increments of 100 she counted. The number was reaching such mega-proportions that my ears began to ring with panic, never having heard such high numbers associated with *my* bank account.

When Krissy finished, she carefully regained my gaze in the mirror. "What do you think it's for?" She whispered hoarsely.

"I don't have any idea!" I stated wide-eyed.

"Wait!" Krissy enthusiastically shouted. "There's a piece of paper!"

Krissy's eyes shone with tears of wonder as she looked at the paper then looked at me.

"Eric!" She told me, "It says here, 'He is Jehovah-Jireh' (which means the Lord will provide), and Eric . . ." she paused and collected herself. "Eric, there is a picture . . . of a *ring!*"

Only God knew of my need. Only God heard our many prayers. And still to this day, only God knows who placed that envelope in my coat pocket. When I get to heaven I'm going to give that person a great big hug!

The Plan

—eric—

the great adventure began with a call to my four parents. Rich and Janet had requested some time to pray about what I asked them over the phone the morning of April 10th. I hung up the phone with an understanding that they would call me back that afternoon with an answer. Less than three minutes later my phone rang. It was Rich.

"Eric," Rich declared, "Janet and I knelt down to pray, looked at each other, and realized we already knew the answer to your question." Rich paused to stir the adrenaline in my veins. Then with a paternal tenderness he said, "We believe it's time!"

My parents were bouncing off the walls when I told them.

"I'm sensing that it's time to propose to Leslie!" I confidently stated with the phone against my ear. "What do you guys think?"

"I'm ready for grandkids!" my mom spouted, "I've felt it was time for two years!"

"Barb!" my dad corrected, "Let's be a little bit more deliberate about this decision. We don't want Eric and Leslie rushing something just so you can have your grandkids!"

"What's there to deliberate, Win?" My mom chimed in. "I think this whole thing is just dripping with God and His goodness. And Eric knows I'm joking! Don't you, hon?"

"Of course I do!" I laughed.

"Have you talked to Rich and Janet yet?" my dad questioned.

"Yeah!" I responded with a chuckle. "They knelt down to pray about it this morning, sort of looked at each other, shook their heads in agreement, and called me back to say that they thought it was time as well!"

"Well, if you can't already tell, Eric," my dad cheered, "I think your mother and I are pretty confident it is time, too!"

———

It wasn't but a couple of days later that I hatched "the plan." "The plan" was full of creatively manufactured circumstances—some seemingly impossible—that would set the stage for "the moment." "The moment" was the precise instant in time when I would say the one word that would leave Leslie breathless and begging to know how I had so mysteriously appeared out of thin air. First, I somehow had to travel from Michigan to Leslie's colorado living room without her realizing I had even left my cozy home. Second, I had to plant clues that would take her off my scent and convince her that some other great event was taking place the very night I would appear. And third, I had to pray. Because Leslie passionately believed that it was absolutely impossible to ever surprise her. And up to that point in her life, she was convinced that no one had ever succeeded in pulling the wool over her eyes.

All my life I had dreamed of this opportunity—to gallantly stroll into a beautiful young woman's life, kneel before her, and ask her to marry me. Over and over I had to pinch myself as I cruised due west on I-90 heading for my princess. I cried, I laughed, I prayed, and I rehearsed my lines. As I drove along in my faithful Toyota Camry, I wrote a poem that would share my heart, my mind, and my soul with this precious woman I loved and adored. As I spoke it outloud in the car I wept with gratefulness. As I uttered the last line I found myself weeping with joy. *This is it!* I said to myself. *I can't believe this is happening to me!*

At seven twenty-eight P.M., April 25th, I stood outside the

Runkles' house holding a dozen roses in one hand and a little white box in the other—waiting for one of the most anticipated moments of my entire life to unfold. The neighbors next door told me later that they were convinced Leslie was standing on the other side of the door unwilling to let me in and I was trying to butter her up with flowers.

Rain pitter-pattered off my head, but absolutely nothing could dampen my reverie and excitement. I slipped out of my rain-moistened loafers, realizing that they might squeak when I attempted to silently tip-toe across the wood floor like an Indian sneaking up on a sleeping desperado.

Lord, may you receive glory tonight! I whispered. I took a few gigantic breaths to try and slow my heart rate. The moments passed with gulps, silent prayers, and a few more deep breaths. I rehearsed my lines inside my restless mind. I stared at the big brass knocker on the blue front door, painstakingly reading the phrase "the Runkles family" over and over and over again. I imagined Leslie inside, the woman I loved. I could envision her soft brown hair gently resting on her shoulders. I could see in my mind's eye her delicate cheeks flushed with surprise. And I could picture her tender emerald eyes brimming with tears of joy. I was ready to see her and express my deepest longings. Then finally . . . the door opened.

The Moment
April 25, 1994

O kay, Leslie," my dad tenderly spoke as my mom dimmed the lights, "just sit on the couch and close your eyes, we're going outside to get your gift."

I sat waiting alone in the living room with my eyes closed while my parents made a few rustling noises around the room. As I heard them close the front door, my mind raced with curiosity. Why would they have to go *outside* to get my gift? And why would my parents give me a present in April when my birthday wasn't for another eight months? Not to mention the fact that the whole thing had seemed spur-of-the-moment, and my mom and dad weren't usually the spontaneous types.

"We've been waiting many years to give you this gift," they had told me at dinner that night. Obviously it was something important for my parents to make such an occasion out of this presentation. I began to wish Eric could be here to share in whatever it was. But then, lately I had found myself *always* wanting Eric near.

Just a couple of days ago, I had sat in the Ludy kitchen across from Barb and Win as we excitedly planned a train-trip to Michigan to visit Eric and Krissy in June. For a while, the knowledge that I would soon be with him made my heart giddy with anticipation. But this morning I had awakened with depression looming over me like a drizzly fog. The days stretched endlessly out before me like a vast blue ocean. June seemed years away. How much longer could I stand not being with Eric? He was not only my very best friend, he was the man I loved so deeply I wanted to share the rest of my life with him.

I gave a thoughtful little laugh as I sat in the deserted living room. Yes, I told myself with a smile, I loved Eric Ludy with all my heart. I had loved him for the past two-and-a-half years since the journey of our friendship first began, and yet, what had started out as a small seed of affection had been nurtured and strengthened over the years. I was suddenly aware that the tiny seed had blossomed into a full-grown, mature rose of true, unending love.

We had never once spoken the words "I love you" to each other. There were so many times I longed to hear him say that one cherished phrase, but somehow we both knew it just wasn't time yet. Eric did his best to make it clear through his letters and phone calls and the little things he did how much he cared for me. But lately, it wasn't the same as hearing him tell me.

My mind drifted back to a scene from the past. Eric and I had been sitting together in the Ludy family room, not long after we met. Somehow we had gotten onto the discussion of romance and relationships.

"I won't say 'I love you,' to a girl unless I'm going to ask her to marry me in the next breath," Eric had declared passionately that night.

Even now, I knew he would stick to his commitment, no matter what. He wanted me to know that when he spoke those precious words to me, it was more than a feeling or emotion . . . it was a commitment for life.

A tender smile played on my lips as my mind dwelled on Eric. I couldn't seem to stop thinking of him, no matter what the situation.

All at once, a soft strain of music began to fill the air. *My parents must have put background music on before they went outside,* I told myself. My heart melted as I instantly recognized the beautiful melody . . . *How Beautiful!* Sentimental tears flowed down my face as my desire for Eric grew even stronger. My parents had chosen the perfect song to play on an important night, and at the very moment I was thinking about *him!* Touched by their thoughtfulness, I tried to still the ache that was longing for Eric.

Suddenly I heard a stirring in the room and the soft whisper of my name, "Leslie."

My eyes flew open as I recognized that unmistakable voice. *Eric!* I sat gaping at him, my face frozen in a mask of utter shock. Questions whirled chaotically through my mind like a gusty hurricane. *How could he possibly be here? I just talked to him on the phone last night in Michigan! What is going on?*

My breath caught in my throat as I watched the man I loved move toward me slowly. I was speechless, enraptured by the magical feelings that flooded over me.

The room had been transformed while I'd had my eyes closed. My parents had dimmed the lights, lit candles, placed flowers all around, started background music . . . then disappeared. As my eyes drank in the strength of Eric's tender gaze, time stood still. In this eternity of such beauty, wonder, mystery, and power, I sat breathless with expectation. Never before had I known anything like it. Moments earlier I had been sitting in a simple living room. Now, I was in a divine sanctuary of the purest love and joy imaginable. We were the only two people on earth.

I watched in quiet wonder as Eric slowly knelt at my feet and carefully reached for a bowl of water and a towel that had been left for him. He gently removed my sandals, and looked into my eyes with a love so intense it made me catch my breath. In the stillness of that moment, words had no place. He lowered my feet into the basin and delicately bathed them, as tears streamed down his face, mingling with the warm water.

Emotion overtook me like the current of a mighty river. I began to weep as I experienced his humble statement of absolute devotion. We'd had many conversations about the symbolism of foot washing. Our Lord Jesus had washed the feet of His bride, the church, just before He laid down His very life for her. We had talked about how we wanted to follow His example. Eric was making a profound commitment to me through this action of washing my feet. He was, in essence, saying, "I choose to serve you and seek your highest good. I want to always love you as Christ loves His bride. I will lay down my life for you."

This was not merely a man full of passion proposing to the woman he loved. This was a man full of the supernatural and sacrificial love of the Lord Jesus Christ, offering himself fully to me, for a lifetime. I could almost hear angels singing with delight. The room seemed filled with the very presence and pleasure of Almighty God.

Eric took my trembling hands in his. Softly he spoke for the first time since he had whispered my name. It was a poem he had written and memorized. It spoke of the great love of the Author of our relationship and the life He was calling us to. As he came to the conclusion he said, "*I love you*, my girl Leslie. Will you marry me?"

He *loved me!* I had been aware of that amazing fact for two long years, but finally hearing the precious words flow sweetly from his lips seemed to seal the boundless depth of that love. I was transformed into a princess. I had never felt more cherished. My heart soared. In all my childhood fairy tale fantasies, I never could have dreamed up a moment more beautiful than this.

Six Months

—eric—

a man in love is a safety hazard. I think a good part of my brain disappeared during the following six months after she said, "Yes! I will marry you, Eric Winston Ludy!" For instance, I locked my keys in the car—and if you knew me you would know how impossible that is. I left my car lights on and ran down the battery. I left the front door to my parents' house open all night after returning from a romantic walk with my little emerald-eyed sweetheart. I even doodled hearts on my teaching notebook during class as my students were taking a test. My mom called it "smitten," my students called it "really weird," my brother called it "black-mail material," and the phone company called it "lucrative."

"I love you!" I warbled into the phone sounding strangely similar to Pee-Wee Herman. "I love you! I miss you! I love you! I miss you! Oh, did I tell you how much I love you?"

The weeks crawled along like a turtle in quicksand. I ached with the desire to be married—to call Leslie my wife. "This is Leslie, my fiancée!" was definitely a step up from "this is my good friend, Leslie." But it was still unfulfilling. I wanted to be married. I wanted to spend my life with her—sharing both sunsets *and* sunrises. I hated goodbyes. Each time I had to leave, the ache would grow more intense. Each time I drove away and saw tears streaming down her soft cheeks, my threshold for patience became thinner.

Our love was deepening and maturing—and challenged. As Leslie grew more familiar with me, she began to ask questions about my past.

"I don't want to talk about it!" I would always say with irritation in my voice.

"Please!" she would beckon with her puppy-dog eyes on display.

"It's hard for me to re-live what took place," was my answer to her pleadings.

With that she took my hand and squeezed it. "It's alright, Eric, if you don't feel comfortable talking about it."

But I knew I needed to talk. I wanted Leslie to know who I was before Jesus changed me. I was scared to let her see the "old" Eric, but I felt strongly that she needed to realize I hadn't always loved her and been faithful to her.

"Uh, . . . Les?" I said one day while sitting on her parent's couch. "I . . . ah, . . . need to tell you something." My eyes awkwardly glanced to and fro and I fidgeted with my baseball cap.

She moved in close, realizing I could use some moral support, and gently placed her arm around my shoulder.

I told her about the girls of my life. When detail was required, I painfully supplied it. When vagueness was requisite, I gladly complied. My heart trembled as I spoke, knowing that this incriminating information would be good reason for Leslie to throw her ring back at me in disgust and never talk to me again.

In retrospect, I would have to say that conversation was one of the most difficult I have ever been involved in. When I saw tears in Leslie's eyes as I mentioned my physical relationship with Laura LaTourno, my heart did a nosedive within my rib cage. I was angry with myself, full of shame and regret. If I had only known how much my decisions back then would impact this precious woman in my life today.

Leslie asked me heights, weights, hair color, shoe size, even what perfume they wore. I could see her self-consciously comparing herself to what I was attracted to in my earlier years. And no matter how many times I told her that they didn't hold a place in my heart, and that her beauty far surpassed theirs, I couldn't take away her pain.

"Les!" I pleaded with tears of my own gracing my cheeks. "I'm sorry! I'm so sorry!"

As the pain-filled minutes passed, we cried in each other's arms. Then with the tenderness of an angel, Leslie whispered in my ear, "Eric, I forgive you! I love you!"

———

Whenever you bare your soul to a friend you easily filter out Christ's love from human love. Only Christ's love can forgive and move on. Only Christ's love can stare into the face of a caterpillar and see a butterfly.

Though insecurities still arose in our love, we found that each and every time we faced head-on a past boyfriend or girlfriend, shared a moral weakness, or simply admitted a difference of opinion, we drew closer. When we encountered each other without masks, our love only grew higher and took deeper root.

The past is hard to face for many of us. Regrets line the misdirected paths we chose to take, like bleached bones on a war-torn battlefield. When I was a teenager, I chose to be molded by the arrogance and ignorance of Donny Lucero rather than the tenderness and wisdom of the Creator of the Universe. But now, over four years since my life was forever changed, the metallic *wham* of locker number 215 seemed like thunder from a distant storm. The heartless words I had stabbed my family with now seemed like lines from a movie from long ago—they couldn't possibly have flowed from *my* lips, could they?

But in my transformation from selfish boy to smitten fiancée, there was still a puzzle piece that was missing. I didn't know it at the time, but my dad held the missing fragment.

eric," my dad said as he led me through the doorway into his bedroom, "why don't you take a seat next to your mother."

I mentally rubbed my eyes to help digest what was taking place. Four chairs were arranged in a small circle at the foot of my parents' bed. My mom was smiling as I entered her room. She patted the seat next to her where I was supposed to sit. There was a seat for my dad, and then one dedicated solely to a box of . . . Kleenex.

My dad closed his bedroom door and carefully made his way into our intimate circle and took his seat. After clearing his throat and studying both my mom and me, he haltingly began.

"Eric," he started then took a deep breath to try and quiet his nerves, "I have typed out something over the past couple of days that I want to read to you." He uncomfortably fidgeted with the piece of white paper in his hand and shifted in his chair.

"There are a lot of things I've needed to say to you for some time," he said while opening up the folded paper. "I don't know how far I will make it through this . . ." he paused while holding in a powerful surge of emotion in his chest.

I stared at my dad in amazement. Never had I seen him go to such lengths to communicate. Never had I seen him so vulnerable to his feelings.

"That's why I have this box of Kleenex," he stated trying to make the moment a bit lighter with a smile.

It was then that the man I had always known as Darth Vadar on life-support when it came to emotions, began to read his white piece of paper. And his words were like iron to my backbone and nobility to my manhood.

"Eric, my son, . . ." his eyes filled with tears and his voice began to falter, "I . . . love you!"

I hadn't heard those words since I was eleven. I always knew he loved me, but something magical was stored up in those special words as my dad spoke them to me with tears dripping down his cheeks.

He continued on, asking forgiveness for his workaholism, his absence at key times growing up when I needed him, and his inability to tell me how proud he was to be my dad.

"I'm so proud of you, son!" I remember him saying near the end of that memorable night. "And I just want you to know, . . . I see you as a *man!*"

Up to that point, God had done so many things in my life. He had changed me in so many ways. But I was still an insecure little boy when it came to the thought of caring for and loving a wife. It was my dad who let me know I could do it.

"Eric," he said to me as we stood up to give hugs, "I know many men, but few that no how to love a woman." He paused and looked into my salty eyes. "You're going to be a great husband Eric, I'm confident in that . . . because you know Jesus!"

If a Chinese sage were going to summarize what I learned in those six months leading up to my wedding, he would have said something like: *man engaged to woman is man with big smile and low resistance to temptation.*

So as not to cause any of you readers to use your imaginations any more than you may have already , I will attempt to summarize in vague generalities instead of specifics. My hands, my eyes, and my lips felt imprisoned like a caged lion and were screaming to be free.

But if it had been important for me to love my future wife faithfully even before I knew her, it was all the more so now that I knew her name and was counting the days until we would finally say "I do."

When you withhold certain physical expressions until marriage it does two things. First, it makes those intimate forms of touch far more appealing to the mind than maybe they otherwise would be. And second, it makes those tender expressions far more enjoyable when the time finally arrives that you are free to enjoy them.

It's the simple principle of waiting. When you wait for something rather than satisfy your craving for it at the genesis of your desire, you appreciate its beauty far more and enjoy its pleasure forever—as opposed to having its appeal fade away.

Let it suffice to say, while waiting was certainly difficult, the reward was far beyond my wildest imagination.

My engagement to Leslie was a once in a lifetime experience. Our love was new, our discovery of each other was fresh and exciting, and our expectancy was bigger than life. I wouldn't want to relive those painful yet amazing days leading up to the wedding, but I certainly will always look back on them with a fondness that is saved only for my very favorite memories.

W hose underwear is on the coffee table?" Barb demanded, her eyes suspiciously examining the white stack of Fruit-of-the-Looms.

"It's mine!" Win hollered from the bedroom, then added, "It's clean!" just in case anyone was wondering.

"Daddy!" Krissy reprimanded his indiscreet remark with a delicately shocked expression on her angelic face. She hurried over to where I was quietly waiting by the front door.

"Don't worry, Leslie, Eric will be out really soon—"

"HEY!" interrupted a loud yelp from the hallway. "MY SHIRT! I just spilled mustard on my favorite SHIRT! Could somebody HELP me over here or something?!" Mark was protesting the fate of his spoiled garment at an ear-splitting volume so that anyone within fifty yards was obligated to cease conversation and give full attention to his latest clothing catastrophe.

Krissy, I had learned over the years, was always the perfect comforter and sympathizer for this kind of plight. "I'll get some baking soda!" she proclaimed heroically, rushing into the bathroom. "It works on mustard every time!"

"HURRY!" Mark bellowed as if his appendix were about to explode.

"Win!" Barb pleaded as she maneuvered through the room dragging a metal ironing board. "Come get your *underwear* off the *coffee* table!"

To add to the confusion, the phone began ringing shrilly.

"Will somebody get that please?" Win commanded, his voice

muffled from his hidden location in one of the back bedrooms.

"KRISSY! MY SHIRT!" Mark's panicked cry resounded once more from the hallway.

I took a hesitant look at the bedlam surrounding the Ludy hotel room. Smiling in amusement, I realized that it had been a while since I'd had the opportunity of witnessing a Ludy-scene in full-gear. During the past year, the Ludy clan had been scattered; Barb and Win having traveled overseas for several months, Krissy teaching in Michigan with Eric, and Mark away at art school in Hawaii. Their lovely house had been sold before the trip abroad, so they had all gathered in a hotel suite a few miles from my house for the wedding festivities this week. Typical Ludy humor, enthusiasm, noise and chaos was back in full swing now that they were all together again (with the exception of Mary the cat who had met her unfortunate end on the bumper of a passing van one unsuspecting afternoon).

The phone continued to blare as all Ludys present scurried about their individual missions.

"Hello?" I finally picked up the receiver, plugging my other ear against the noisy scene around me.

"Hi, this is Joan, the caterer for the rehearsal dinner tonight! I need to know if you want twenty pasta primaveras and ten chicken cacciatoris or the other way around!"

"Uh, hold on a minute." I placed my hand over the mouthpiece and searched the hallway for Barb.

"It's for you," I handed her the phone as she exited the bathroom with a teal can of Magic Sizing.

"Hellooooo!" she sang cheerfully into the receiver. "No, Joan, we decided on the chocolate mousse for dessert, not the five layer iced cake! Okay, well, I'll be right over as soon as I get my blouse ironed!"

Eric finally emerged from one of the bedrooms wearing jeans, a hunter green sweatshirt, and a dark blue baseball cap.

"Just think," he whispered mischievously, walking over to me and taking my hand, "in just two days . . . you'll be a Ludy, too!"

"Anyone seen my underwear lately?" Win questioned, standing over the coffee table looking confused.

"I think Mommy threw them in the laundry pile!" Krissy offered, coming into the kitchen with a dripping wet blue shirt. "She didn't want them on the coffee table," Krissy informed him sincerely.

"No kidding!" Win sighed in frustration.

"I'm LATE!" Mark howled from the hallway.

"Coming!" Krissy resounded, frantically trying to air-dry Mark's now-saved shirt.

"Who moved the ironing board?" Barb begged, having momentarily been put on hold by Joan.

I glanced at Eric with a weary smile. "Let's go," I said in mock exhaustion. Eric just laughed as he held the door for me.

―

Just think what family reunions will be like in ten years with that bunch!" he joked as we stepped into the main walkway outside.

I laughed good-naturedly as he closed the door behind us.

"You nervous?" he smiled down at me.

"About becoming a Ludy, you mean?" I questioned, smiling. "No, I think it will be great to get a little Ludy 'wildness' in my blood!"

Eric chuckled at my remark. "I mean," he explained, "are you worried about the wedding?"

"Well, a little, I guess. I've been working on the details for so long I just . . . hope it all goes okay!" I floundered, taking a deep breath to quiet the churning in my stomach. *Calm down*, I commanded myself, *the wedding's still two days away!*

Eric nodded in understanding and tenderly placed his arm around my shoulder as we approached the elevator.

"The last six months sure have flown by," he recalled while pressing his thumb on the down button.

My mind quickly rewound back to all that had happened since that unforgettable night in April when Eric had asked me to marry him. . . .

a fter a whirlwind day of picking out a wedding set and visiting close friends to announce our engagement, Eric had flown back to Michigan to finish out the rest of the school year, leaving the beloved Toyota Camry in my faithful care.

With an engagement ring on my finger and unspeakable joy in my heart, saying goodbye was difficult but bearable. I knew I would be spending three incredible weeks with Eric and his family in just two months. In the meantime I poured myself into my new secretarial job and began the wedding preparations.

We decided on December as the month we would be married because Eric would be able to take nearly three weeks off from teaching for our honeymoon.

"And besides," I had reminded him on the phone that night with an open calendar on my lap, "December is the month we first met. It's also the month of our birthdays! So why not stick an anniversary in there too?"

"Sure, why not!" he enthusiastically agreed. We'd set the date for December 10th.

I smiled as I remembered my overwhelming anticipation as the

Amtrak train had crept into the Kalamazoo train station early one Saturday morning in June, six months prior. Grabbing my suitcases, I charged past the other drowsy passengers and rushed onto the platform where Eric was waiting for me with a huge grin and a warm enveloping hug.

That visit had been amazing. Krissy, Barb, Win, Eric and I spent a week in Michigan, then once more boarded the train for a two-week tour of Massachusetts, New Hampshire, Maine, New Brunswick, and up onto Prince Edward Island. Eric and I were helplessly in love and beyond ecstatic to be together. Our excitement matched that of small children right before presents on Christmas morning.

It seemed that God had unlocked our hearts completely, and the floodgates of romance and passion had finally been released. The emotions were so strong. I realized how grateful I was that we had saved this stage of our relationship until now. If I hadn't had the knowledge that we would be married soon, I doubt I could have handled the intense longings that washed over me each time we were together.

I recalled a gorgeous scene on Prince Edward Island as Eric and I had walked along a deserted beach, hand-in-hand, observing a glorious hue of crimson over the mountains in the distance. Wind whipped at our hair and clothes and sand sifted between our bare toes as white foamy waves crashed onto the shore.

"This is where *Anne of Green Gables* must have been filmed!" Eric excitedly informed me as we studied the glorious nature around us. *Anne of Green Gables* was our favorite romantic movie. Eric couldn't hold back tears whenever he saw the scene where Anne and Gilbert kiss on the bridge in the end of the story. (At times, I think he lived vicariously through Gilbert.)

We walked together silently for a few moments, afraid to break the romantic spell. Finally, we approached a huge flat rock. Eric quickly jumped up on it and offered me a hand. As I sat beside him on the cold gray surface, he looked deeply into my eyes with an intimate gaze only the two of us could ever understand. I was mesmerized by the tenderness and desire I saw within his expression. We sat gazing at each other for several minutes, breathless and spellbound by the surge of love between us. Slowly, as if in a dream, he moved his face closer to mine. Then leaning forward, he gently brushed his cheek against mine. And softly he kissed me—almost.

Just before his lips brushed mine, he pulled away, cleared his throat, and sighed.

"Sometimes this drives me crazy, Les," he said, raking a hand through his brown curls in frustration. "I mean, are you still glad we decided not to kiss till our wedding day?"

I chuckled softly, feeling the passionate tension of the moment ease away as I turned and faced the vast ocean scene below us.

"Well, if we end up kissing before then, I don't think God will mind," I offered teasingly. "It's just that . . . in my past, I kissed so many guys carelessly when it didn't even mean anything at all. A kiss was so . . . cheapened. But with you, I really want it to be the purest, most special, most meaningful kiss in the world!" I stopped and smiled up at him, admiring the cute trademark mole above the left side of his mouth. "I think it will be really fun if we are able to save our first kiss for the wedding ceremony!"

The next two weeks were full of romantic walks, passionate talks, dreaming about our future together, and a healthy dose of emotional gush. But we were always careful not to allow ourselves to be alone together for too long. The longing to express our love physically was growing stronger by the day. And as our desire grew, so did the temptation to compromise in ways beyond just kissing.

We spent plenty of time around Eric's family, and made ourselves accountable to them.

———

I giggled suddenly as I was reminded of the train ride home to Colorado that summer.

Eric turned to me quizzically as we stepped inside the elevator.

"Do you remember the train ride?" I asked playfully as he pressed his pointer finger on the *L* for Lobby.

A rueful expression crept over his face. "Oh, you mean when my parents missed the train in Boston?" he shook his head incredulously at the memory.

At the end of that memorable vacation with Eric's family, Win had dropped Krissy, Eric and me off at the train station while he and Barb made their way through rush-hour traffic to return the rental car. Soon it had become obvious that they were going to miss the train. The three of us had had no choice but to board without them. After the first few hours, Krissy had to exit at her stop in Chicago. It was then that Eric and I realized we had only one sleeper car between the two of us for the rest of the 30-hour ride back to Denver.

"Remember how that porter thought you were crazy?" I reminded him laughing.

"Yeah! How many guys would actually want to give up the opportunity to spend the night in a private room with a beautiful girl?"

"Well," I recalled, "it was certainly nice of you to give me that big sleeper car all to myself!"

"Yeah," he replied rolling his eyes in mock disgust. "I NEVER want to be stuck sleeping in the observation car again! I had a backache for a week!" He looked down at me teasingly. "It would have been a lot more fun to stay in that sleeper car with you!" he added lightly.

I laughed. "Well, that's one temptation I'm very glad we didn't give in to!"

He nodded thoughtfully as the elevator gently lowered us to the main level and the doors slid open. "That's for sure. Next week is going to the most incredible honeymoon two people ever had!" His eyes sparkled at me teasingly as he fidgeted in his pocket for the car keys. We slowly made our way across the lobby. "Sometimes I thought we'd never make it to the wedding, Les," he confessed. "A few times I seriously considered asking you if you just wanted to elope!"

"And miss walking down the aisle in my beautiful dress?" I looked at him in mock horror.

We walked through a set of revolving glass doors, stepped into the parking lot and squinted against the bright morning sun. I found myself reminiscing about all the long months leading up to this long awaited week of our wedding. . . .

⌒

after the train trip home, Eric had spent the remainder of the summer working for a family friend about six hours away. I dove wholeheartedly into "wedding stuff," trying on bridal gowns, visiting churches and reception halls, and picking invitations.

Before we knew it, August had arrived and Eric was off for his second year of teaching in Michigan.

"How many more times am I going to have to say goodbye to you?" I had whispered tearfully as we sat together in the airport.

"I pray this will be the last time," he comforted, smoothing a strand of hair away from my forehead.

The fall months had dragged by with agonizing slowness. I kept as busy as possible with my job, wedding plans, and various kinds of ministry. But there were more than a few nights I cried myself to sleep, comforting myself with the reminder that in just a few months, God willing, I would be snuggled in bed next to my wonderful husband.

———

So, what time do I need to be at the tux shop tomorrow?" Eric questioned, jarring me back to the present.

I slid into the passenger's side of the Camry and reached for my Daytimer. "Um, let's see . . . oh, here it is. They're expecting you and the rest of the groomsmen at two o'clock." I narrowed my eyes at him. "And don't forget!" I commanded fiercely. "It took me about twenty phone calls to get that whole thing set up!"

Eric grinned at my abrupt seriousness. "Don't worry," he replied confidently.

We plodded through an exhausting day of final wedding details. During the hour-long rehearsal the groomsmen entered at the wrong time and the pianist forgot his music. Then we sat through an emotionally charged rehearsal dinner full of sentimental speeches. We dabbed our napkins to our eyes as we secured the wholehearted endorsement of our friends and family on our new life together. Eric finally dropped me off at my house. We had planned several months ago to have the rehearsal two days before the wedding, so we wouldn't need to be together at all before the big day. I wanted the moment when I walked down the aisle to be as dramatic as possible!

He took my hand as we walked slowly up to the house. I paused on my front porch and turned to face him.

"Bye," I whispered gently, "see you at the wedding."

He gazed at me tenderly then spoke quietly. "After tomorrow, Les," he observed with tears shining in his brown eyes, "we won't have to say goodbye anymore!"

The Day a Dream Came True
December 10th, 1994

—eric—

I will be waiting for you at the head of the aisle.
With tears in my eyes, and on my lips a smile.

Those were the words I wrote her. "Don't open it until the morning of the wedding!" I had carefully instructed.

—

i stared into the bowl of fruit elaborately situated on the foldout table in the groom's dressing room. I couldn't eat; my stomach was absent from my body. I was one giant heart in love. A sense of Christmas morning mixed with a thousand Easters and Thanksgivings filled the air. I was floating. Christmas music played in the background and wedding bells chimed in my heart. Even orange and neon pink would have looked good together on this day.

"Eric?" Marky crashed into my dreamland, "What does it feel like?" He set his strong hand on my shoulder and squeezed.

"I don't think there are words for it!" I stated with a smile plastered all over my face.

"Well, for what it's worth—I'm excited for you!" Marky offered with a gigantic smile of his own.

"Thanks, Marky!" I laughed and reached out to give him a bear hug. "I'm gonna miss ya!"

—

he feeling of expectancy was like kernels of unpopped popcorn waiting in the bubbling oil to burst forth into a new life. I couldn't think of anything but my bride. Everything else was meaningless outside of her. I ached with anticipation wishing I could fast-forward to the moment I would say, "I will and I do!" I was ready to love her. Ready to serve her. Ready to care for her.

"Five minutes!" Marky smiled. "It's only five minutes away!"

"Could we pray?" I found myself asking.

Soon all the available men in the groom's dressing room huddled into a circle and held hands.

"Lord," Pastor Craig prayed, "Eric and Leslie have allowed you to write a beautiful love story on their behalf. Now Jesus, please be the guest of honor at this covenant-sealing event!"

"Father, may Your sweet presence be here tonight," my dad pleaded, "and may you be honored and glorified through Eric and Leslie's love and commitment."

"God, we thank you for your amazing faithfulness in Eric and Leslie's lives." Rich reverently uttered. "Bring to completion what you have so perfectly begun!"

"Jesus," Marky added, "please bless my brother for his willingness to follow You and let You lead."

"Lord," I concluded, "may this entire event turn eyes and hearts to see You in all Your majesty and all Your glory! May the world see that Your ways are perfect!"

—

'll never forget standing outside of the candle-lit sanctuary, waiting for my musical cue to enter. *Tears and a smile*, I thought to myself, *I promised Leslie tears and a smile*.

In those moments prior to walking out before the large crowd of witnesses, it seemed time temporarily ceased. God's peace filled me and He made me lie down in a green pasture of stillness and contemplation. Scenes from my past flooded my mind and reminded me of the graciousness and love of my sweet Jesus.

I thought of my many mistakes with girls—my many slides into the black cauldron of lust and impurity. I thought of my terrible attitude towards my family and how many times I had injured those that loved me most and best. I thought about Jesus and how I had turned away from His love and sought the love of this world. But then I saw a picture of a gorgeous young woman who loved me and accepted me. I didn't deserve such a prize from God. I wasn't worthy of such a gift of beauty. But this amazing woman loved me. Me—of all people! In such a crystal clear way I could sense the love of Jesus—loving me even though I'm so unlovable. How humbled I felt as I stood waiting in the darkened room just outside the glorious stained-glass sanctuary.

"Thank you my precious Lord!" I whispered. "Thank you for your forgiveness, your new life, and your perfect faithfulness."

Then the music started that heralded my entrance. "Here I come, Leslie!" I silently mouthed. "I'll be waiting for you at the head of the aisle with tears and a smile!"

I carefully took my first step into the heavenly sanctuary—the wind of the Spirit of God greeting me. My heart melted as I saw the vast crowd sitting silently in their pews. Faces I knew well. Some I hadn't seen in many years. A well of emotion churned inside me and forced its way to my throat. I swallowed hard, attempting to harness the Herculean emotional pressure within my chest. In front of everyone I knew, my eyes spilled over with tears and my chest heaved with sobs.

For so many years I had waited for this day—and here it finally was. This moment was real. It wasn't imagined and it wasn't something out of a movie that would suddenly disappear with the final credits. This was genuine beauty. Genuine perfection. The genuine love of God.

Tears and a smile, I thought to myself. My face was riddled with emotion and my lips were impossible for me to control. *A smile*, I commanded myself, *a smile!*

The moment had arrived. My bride was ready to enter. *A smile*, I told my tear-filled face, *a smile!*

The bridal procession started. Everyone stood and awaited the priceless moment Leslie would enter. If beauty could be measured by delight, then never has there been a more beautiful bride in all of the world's history. It was only when her gracious presence entered the candlelit room that my tears stopped flowing and my lips were free to express the measureless joy bubbling in my heart. When I saw my princess holding tightly to the secure arm of her father, I gave her a smile. A smile blended with tears of joy that I don't think she or I will ever forget.

The Day a Dream Came True
December 10, 1994

—leslie—

Y ou're going to do great Les," my dad smiled comfortingly, placing a steadying hand on my shaking arm.

"I think I'm going to faint," I whispered, pursing my lips together nervously.

He chuckled softly. "Don't faint."

We stood together behind the huge double doors, waiting for our cue to enter the sanctuary. My breath was coming in short, shallow gasps. It took all my willpower to force myself to stop my violent trembling.

Lord, I have waited for this day my entire life, I silently pleaded, *please give me peace to make it through the ceremony! Let me cherish this moment, not be distracted by my nerves.*

Suddenly, I heard a thunderous noise and I realized the audience was slowly standing to their feet. A beautiful strain of music filled the air and I recognized our cue. We waited as the massive wooden doors were opened, then carefully stepped into the candlelit sanctuary. With one tender look at my dad, I placed my foot onto the white runner and began moving forward, yards of silky satin swishing around me.

The moment I took that first step down the aisle, my loving father by my side, I was flooded with a sense of indescribable peace, wonder, and awe that I have never before or since experienced.

I moved toward the front of the church as if in a dream. At first, my eyes scanned the rows of hundreds of friends and family gazing at me with tender smiles. But as my dad and I approached the halfway mark, I was finally able to catch a glimpse of my groom. He was waiting for me at the head of the aisle, his body rigid with emotion. Tears were streaming unheeded down his face. His eyes were fastened only on me. And as I lifted my quivering chin to meet his gaze, his face broke into an enormous smile of pure delight.

Tears and a smile, I reminded myself joyfully, *he is waiting for me with tears and a smile!*

As my father joined my hand with Eric's, he uttered the words, "Eric, Janet and I now give to you . . . our daughter . . . to love, to care for, and to protect." My dad's voice broke with emotion and I fought back the urge to give way to the river of sentimental tears that threatened to spill down my cheeks.

As Eric took my hands in his own, I felt a strength flow through me. Standing at the altar looking deeply into his eyes, the rest of the world faded away. I was helplessly lost in the depth of my love for him as I stood gazing tenderly into his moist eyes. This was the man I had been waiting for all my life, my prince. And yet, he was so much more than a knight in shining armor . . . he was God's perfect gift to me.

—

t he exuberant pastor had come to the end of the ceremony. I stood facing my husband, a beautiful ring on my finger, love coursing through me like an unstoppable waterfall. And breathlessly, I knew the moment was about to arrive . . . the moment we had both longed for since that unforgettable talk on the grassy hill.

"You may now," the pastor drew the words out dramatically as he smiled at us, "kiss . . . the . . . bride!"

Until that moment in time, a kiss had been merely a sweet

expression of romantic feeling, a symbol of physical desire. But when Eric's soft lips finally met mine on that night in December, a kiss suddenly became so much more. Electricity and warmth surged through me unlike I'd ever known. All at once, the sanctuary was filled with an audience beyond the tearful faces of our faithful family and friends — angels were singing, heaven was cheering! I could feel our Father smiling tenderly, tears of joy falling down His own face. I could hear His gentle whisper, *Well done, my children, well done. You have lived in true purity, and today you have tasted true love.*

As the amazing kiss lingered, my mind flashed back to my childhood—my fairy tale, starry-eyed ideals of what I longed for romance to be. I remembered how I had let those dreams die as I got older, how I had carelessly thrown my heart around, not believing that there was anything better.

Slowly, Eric drew back, and I smiled at him with wonder and amazement. God had given me more than I could ever comprehend. He had restored my innocence. He had lifted me out of the darkness. He had taught me what true faithfulness was about. And yet, on this amazing day before a crowd of many witnesses, it was not my faithfulness or Eric's that shone like a brilliant star for all to see. It was God's unfailing faithfulness to us—two sinners. We had given Him a little handful of pebbles; He had given us a truckload of jewels in return. In this unforgettable moment, He had given us the unsurpassed treasure of true purity, true love, and true romance.

———

euphoria filled me as Eric took me by the arm and led me down the aisle, past the rows of friends and family who stood cheering and dabbing tearfully at their eyes as they watched us.

As we left the emotionally charged sanctuary, Eric swept me into a tiny chapel at the back of the lobby. His strong arms came around me, and we clung to each other, laughing and crying simultaneously with utter joy. Within moments, our family had surrounded us, and the ten of us became a chaotic mass of hugging, weeping, laughing, and rejoicing. This was not just *our* day of triumph. It was *theirs* as well. They had been there for us all along the way, cheering us on, standing beside us, offering us a prayer, a rebuke, or word of counsel whenever we needed it. And these eight special people were now sharing in the victory of our unforgettable day.

---

i t was the purest, most beautiful kiss in the whole world!" I said to Eric softly as we sat together in the back of the limo, riding away from the reception hall. "Aren't you glad we saved it for this day?"

Eric just smiled at me, his face alight with boyish excitement. "It was a moment I'll never forget," he whispered, and kissed me softly again.

As we held each other silently, I sighed in absolute contentment. Every detail of this day had been so perfect.

"So Les," Eric said, cupping my face gently, "would you say this was the day that your dreams came true?"

I thought for a moment, a little smile playing on my lips.

"No," I finally admitted, looking up at him seriously. "My dreams would never compare to what God did between us today." I paused and looked deeply into the adoring eyes of my husband. "No," I said again with conviction. "This was the day that *His* dreams for *us* came true!"

Epilogue
Mr. Valé

after twenty-three years of dreaming about this, imagining what it must be like, watching it in movie theaters, reading about it nearly every time I picked up a newspaper, magazine, or book—my Day arrived, sombrero and all.

I only spent twenty-four hours with him, though he had been waiting since long before I was born to throw me this great fiesta. God created Mr. Valé for one single purpose. It was his life's work to decorate the stage for the most tender and precious of romances. He didn't just do his job well, he was the best I've ever seen. He was a better archer than cupid and a better set-director than anyone in the history of Hollywood.

It was later that night, just before he passed away, that I saw him last. The guests had gone home and I was carefully removing count-less grains of rice from my curly brown hair when he looked at me with reminiscing eyes and whispered in my ear.

"Amigo," he said softly, "God has given you something today that all the money in the world couldn't buy." With tears streaming down his aged cheeks he leaned down and kissed my forehead, "Never forget what God has done for you. And take good care of your princess." With that he turned to leave.

"Uh, wait," I said, "I don't even know your name!"

He paused and answered, "Oh, I'm sorry, didn't you know? I'm The Day A Dream Came True," with that he carefully placed his sombrero on his white head, picked up his cane, yanked up his suitcase full of memories and headed for the door. But then before he strode off into the crimson night sky, he turned, and with that twinkle in his eye he yelled back, "but, Amigo, you can call me Valé la Pena."

"I'm sorry Sir, but I . . . I don't speak Spanish."

He let out one final laugh and then said with all the sweetness of a honey drenched sopapilla, "My dear friend, it simply means, 'it's worth all the pain.'"

What a perfect name. For years I had waited for this Day to arrive. My Day of love; my Day of triumph; my Day of wedded bliss. There were countless times I thought I would never make it, but here I was watching my once in a lifetime Day fade into the night. A tear dripped from my eye and carefully ventured down my cheek. What a Day it was!

"Thank you God!" I whispered with a smile forming on my moistened face. "I'll never forget . . . never!"

Little kids know how to dream. But as we grow up we quickly learn to be careful not to put too much stock in "happily ever after" conclusions. Once upon a time we innocently believed in fairy tale endings to difficult lives. But as we mature, and gain sophistication, we often stop believing in the Heaven at the end of the race, and so strangely dare only to believe in the hell in which we're struggling through today.

Les and I found the pain that inevitably comes when you choose to walk a road less traveled, but we also found the prize. We found the troubles, but we also found the God who turns all our troubles into glorious triumphs. We found loneliness, but we also discovered the wonder of sincere and tender relationships. And along the way we stumbled across an amazing secret . . .the secret to unlocking dreams.

It's actually quite simple really. Somewhere along the way, Leslie and I realized that God's ways are better than our own. But they aren't just better—they're bigger, brighter, bolder, and a million times more beautiful. Our own dreams, formed within our little mortal minds, may seem romantic and surreal. But the dreams of our God that are formed within his eternal all-loving almighty mind are far beyond anything we could ever imagine. Not long ago, on a day when rice filled my hair and inexpressible joy filled my heart . . . He reminded me of His greatness.

Believe me. True love is worth all the pain that patience and perseverance can inflict. You'll have to experience it for yourself, but even something as simple as a kiss becomes unforgettable and priceless when the Author of Romance is scripting the love story. Let me tell you now—God is always near . . . *when dreams come true.*

About the Authors

a s best-selling authors, musicians, and speakers, Eric and Leslie Ludy have spent the past five years working closely with thousands of youth, young adults and singles of all ages. A cutting-edge young couple, Eric and Leslie are widely recognized as a leading voice to the younger generation for their timely message on seeking purity in relationships. Eric and Leslie are the co-founders of RGeneration, a non-profit organization based in Colorado, with the goal of training Christian leaders for the next generation. They have produced two music albums and co-authored four books.